Python programming

2 manuscripts - python crash course, python for data analysis

**By
Dany Log**

Copyright © 2020 by Dany Log

All rights reserved.

The material contained herein is presented with the intent of furnishing pertinent and relevant information and knowledge on the topic with the sole purpose of providing entertainment. The author should thus not be considered an expert on the topic in this material despite any claims to such expertise, first-hand knowledge, and any other reasonable claim to specific knowledge on the material contained herein. The information presented in this work has been researched to ensure its reasonable accuracy and validity. Nevertheless, it is advisable to consult with a duly licensed professional in the area pertaining to this topic, or any other covered in this book, in order to ensure the quality and validity of the advice and/or techniques contained in this material.

This is a legally binding statement as deemed so by the Committee of Publishers Association and the American Bar Association in the United States. Any reproduction, transmission, copying, or otherwise duplication of the material contained in this work are in violation of current copyright legislation. No physical or digital copies of this work, both total and partial, may not be done without the Publisher's express written consent. All additional rights are reserved by the publisher of this work.

The data, facts, and description of events forthwith shall be considered as accurate unless the work is deemed to be a work of fiction. In any event, the Publisher is exempt of responsibility for any use of the information contained in the present work on the part of the user. The Author and Publisher may not be deemed liable, under any circumstances, for the events resulting from the observance of the advice, tips, techniques and any other contents presented herein.

Given the informational and entertainment nature of the content presented in this work, there is no guarantee as to the quality and validity of the information. As such, the contents of this work are deemed as universal. No use of copyrighted material is used in this work. Any references to other trademarks are done so under fair use and by no means represent an endorsement of such trademarks or their holder.

Table of Contents

Python Crash Course 1

Introduction 2
Who is meant to read this book? 2
What will you learn from this book? 2

Chapter 1: Python Programming 4
What is Python Programming? 4
How to use Python Programming 8
Who can use Python Programming? 11
What can you do with Python Programming? 15
Importance of Python Programming in the Economics 19
Importance of Python Programming at the Workplace 21
How can you earn using Python Programming? 25

Chapter 2: Python Programming Concepts 29
Basic Concepts in Python Programming 29
The Terms used in Python Programming 33
How to start Python Programming for Data Analysis .. 41

How to Install Python 44

Chapter 3: Python Programming Lessons 54

How to Learn about Python Programming 54

Where can you learn about Python Programming? 60

What is the Cost of Getting a Python Certification? ... 67

The Best Python Course 68

What Job can you get with Python? 71

Chapter 4: Operating Systems 77

Python on Linux 78

Python on OS X 83

Python on Windows 94

Python Troubleshooting 97

Chapter 5: List 101

What is a List? 101

How to Change Elements 108

How to Remove Element 110

How to Add Elements 115

How to Organize a List 120

Chapter 6: Variable and Simple Data Types 132

Dictionaries 132

Functions 136

Classes 138

Testing your Code 139

File and Exceptions 143

User Input and while Loops 149
Chapter 7: Data Visualization 152
How to Generate Data 152
How to Download Data 159
How to Work with APIs 168
Chapter 8: Web Applications 177
How to Work with Django 181
User Accounts 184
How to Style and Deploy an App 187
Conclusion 190

Python for Data Analysis ... 193

Introduction ... 194

Chapter 1: What is a Data Analysis ... 198

    What is Data Analytics? ... 199

    Understanding How Data Analytics Works ... 202

    The Different Types of Data Analytics ... 206

Chapter 2: Reasons to Work with a Data Analysis ... 211

Chapter 3: How Does Python Fit Into This? ... 222

Chapter 4: Some of the Basic Codes in Python ... 232

    The Keywords ... 233

    Python Comments ... 233

    Python as an OOP Language ... 235

    How to Write a Class ... 237

    Python Functions ... 243

    Python Variables ... 249

    Lists vs. Dictionaries ... 251

    Creating a Simple Loop ... 255

    The If Else Statement in Decision Control ... 256

    Can I Create an Inheritance? ... 260

Chapter 5: What is the NumPy Library ... 266

    Understanding More About NumPy ... 268

Chapter 6: Taking It Further with Pandas 275

How to Install Pandas 277

The Data Structures in Pandas................................... 278

Chapter 7: The Importance of Cleaning and Organizing the Data 283

Collecting the Data 284

Organizing the Data 286

Dealing with the Outliers.. 288

Filling in Missing Data 290

How to Deal with Duplicates 292

Chapter 8: Training, Testing, and Repeating...... 295

Picking Out the Algorithms to Use............................. 296

Training Our Data 300

Testing the Data.. 301

Repeat the Process 305

Chapter 9: Machine Learning and How It Fits Into Our Data Analysis 309

What is Machine Learning? 310

How Does Machine Learning Work with Data Analysis? 315

Supervised Machine Learning.................................... 316

Unsupervised Machine Learning 318

Reinforcement Machine Learning 321

Chapter 10: Presenting the Results 327

Conclusion 341

Python Crash Course

A Complete Step-by-Step Beginner Guide for Python Coding, NumPy, Pandas, and Data Visualization

Introduction

Who is meant to read this book?

This book Python Crash Course: *A Complete Step-by-Step Beginner Guide for Python Coding, NumPy, Pandas, and Data Visualization* is meant for any individual who is interested in Python programming. The experts who want to learn more. For beginners who want to learn everything and other professionals like finance and economy experts. Several individuals would like to earn from Python programming. You will learn all that from the book.

What will you learn from this book?

This book will clearly elaborate on the definition of Python programming, how you can use it, and the people who can benefit from it. There is enough information on what you can do with the information. You will get all the information you need on how important Python programming is to economists and in your workplace. Do you know that you can earn money from Python programming? If your answer is no, do not worry; all the information you need is clearly illustrated.

There are different concepts when it comes to Python programming, on the terms used, how to install Python, the courses offered, and what job you can get with Python skills. There are different operating systems that are used for Python programming like Linux, Windows, and OS X and how you can do troubleshooting. There are different variables and data types like classes, functions, and dictionaries. Data visualization and web applications are chapters that are important to learn and understand. You need to know what the list is, how to change, remove, add elements on the list, and you will know how to organize a list.

Chapter 1: Python Programming

What is Python Programming?

This is a programming language that is objected-oriented and of high level and uses semantics. It is a high level in terms of structures in data and a combination of dynamic typing and binding. This is what makes it attractive to be used for Rapid Application Development and for connecting different elements.

Python with its simplicity and learning with ease helps in reading the programming language, and that is why it reduces the cost to maintain the program. Python encourages the program modularity and code reuse; this is because it supports different packages and modules. The standard library and the Python interpreter can be found in binary form. It is not necessary to charge all the available platforms and can be distributed freely.

Most programmers love the Python program because they offer great productivity. The edit-test debug is a cycle that is fast and does not need any compilation process. It is easier to debug a Python program; it will not cause any segmentation fault. An exception is raised when an error is discovered by the interpreter. When the exception is not known by the program, the interpreter prints a trace. The debugger, on a level of sourcing, will allow being inspecting any variables. There will be a settling of breakpoints, arbitrary expressions, and stepping on the code at any time. The Python is what writes the debugger, the easier, and a quick debugging method and programs of adding prints on the source and statements.

Python is open-source; this means you can use them freely for any commercial applications. Python is programmed to work on UNIX, Windows, and Mac and can be transferred to Java. Python is a language that helps in scripting and helps in web applications for different content.

It is like Perl and Ruby. Python is helped by several imaging programs; users are able to create customized extensions. There are different web applications supporting Python API like Blender and GIMP.

This information given on Python programming is beneficial for both the newbies and the experienced ones. Most of the experienced programmers can easily learn and use Python. There is an easier way to install Python. Most distributors of UNIX and Linux have the recent Python. That is the reason why most computers come already installed with Python. Before you start using Python, you need to know which IDEs and text editors' best work with Python. To get more help and information, you can peruse through introductory books and code samples.

The Python idea was discovered in 1980 after the ABC language. Python 2.0 was introduced, it had features like garbage collection and list comprehensions; which are used in reference cycle collection. When Python 3.0 was released in 2008, it brought about a complete language revision. Python is primarily used for developing software and webs, for mathematics and scripting systems. The latest version of Python is known a Python 3 while Python 2 is still popular. Python was developed to help in reading and similar aspects to different languages like English and emphasis on Mathematics.

A new line is used to complete a Python command, as opposed to other programming languages that normally use semi-colons. It depends on indentation, whitespace, and defining the scope.

How to use Python Programming

Before using Python, you first need to install and run it on your computer, and once you do that, you will be able to write your first program. Python is known as a programming platform that cuts across multiple platforms. You can use it on Linux, macOS, Windows, Java, and .NET machines freely and as an open-source. Most of the Linux and Mac machines come preinstalled even though on an outdated version. That is the main reason why you will need to install the latest and current version.

An easier way to run Python is by using Thonny IDE; this is because it is bundled with the latest version of Python. This is an advantage since you will not need to install it separately. To achieve all that, you can follow the simple steps below:

- ❖ First, you will need to download Thonny IDE
- ❖ Then run the installer in order to install it on your computer

- ❖ Click on File option, then new. Save the file on .py extension, for instance, morning.py or file.py. You are allowed to use any name for the file, as long as it ends with .py. Write the Python code on the file before saving it.
- ❖ To run the file, click on RUN, the run current script. Alternatively, click on F5 in order to run it.

There is also an alternative to install Python separately; it does not involve installing and running Python on the computer. You will need to follow the listed steps below:

- ❖ Look for the latest version of Python and download it.
- ❖ The next step is to run the installer file in order to install Python
- ❖ When installing, look for Add Python to environment variables. This will ensure that Python is added to the environment variables and that will enable you to run Python from any computer destination and part. You have

> the advantage to choose the path to install Python.

❖ When you complete the process of installing, you can now run Python.

There is also an alternative and immediate mode to run Python. When Python is installed, you will type Python on the command line; the interpreter will be in immediate mode. You can type Python code, and when you press enter, you will get the output. For instance, when you type 1 + 1 and then press enter, you will get the output as 2. You can use it as a calculator, and you quit the process, type quit, then press enter.

The second way to do it is by running Python on the Integrated Development Environment. You can use any editing software in order to write the Python script file. All you need to do is to save it the extension .py, and it is considered a lot easier when you use an IDE. The IDE is a feature that has distinctive and useful features like file explorers, code hinting, and syntax checking and highlighting that a programmer can use for application development.

You need to remember that when you install Python, there is an IDE labeled IDLE that will also be installed. That is what you will use to run Python on the computer and it is considered the best IDE for beginners. You will have an interactive Shell when IDLE is opened. This is the point where you can have a new file and ensure that you save it as a .py extension.

Who can use Python Programming?

There is a big challenge out there in choosing a programming language that you can use for your coding businesses. The bigger question is which language are you supposed to learn? Python is a program that is easy to use, and there are known companies that use it. This is one of the reasons why you should adapt to its uses. This is also the reason why worldwide developers have taken advantage.

- ❖ **Google**: Since the beginning of Python, Google has been its supporter. They choose Python because it was easy to maintain it, deploy, and faster in delivery. The first web-crawling spider used for Google was in Java 1.0. It was difficult to use and maintain, and they had to do it again on Python. Python is one of the main programming languages that Google uses, the others include Java, C++, and Go that are used for production. Python is an important part of Google. They have been using it for many years, and it remains a system that is evolving and grows. Many engineers that work for Google prefer using Python. They keep seeking engineers with Python skills.

- ❖ **Facebook**: Production engineers that work for Facebook have a positive comment about Python. This has made Python among the top three programming languages after C++ and

Hack. Facebook adopted Python because it is easy to use. With over 5000 services on Facebook, this is definitely the best programming language. The engineers do not need to maintain or write much coding, and this allows them to focus on live improvements. This is one of the reasons why Facebook infrastructure scales efficiently. Python is used for infrastructure management, for network switch setup, and for imaging.

❖ **Instagram**: From 2016, engineers working for Instagram declared that they were running the biggest Django web framework that was entirely written in Python. The engineers stated that they like Python because of the simple way to use it and how practical it is. That is why the engineers have invested their resources and time in using Python in all their trades. In recent times, Instagram has moved their codes from Python 2.7 to Python 3.

❖ **Spotify**: Spotify is a music-streaming platform that uses Python as its programing language for back end services and data analysis. The reason why Spotify decided to use Python is that they like the way it works in writing and in coding. Spotify will use its analytics in order to offer its users recommendations and suggestions. For the interpretation, Spotify uses Luigi that collaborates with Hadoop. The source will handle the libraries that work together. It will consolidate all the error logs and helps in troubleshooting and redeployment.

- ❖ **Quora:** Before implementing their idea, Quora decided to use Python programming for their question and answer platform. The Quora founders decided to go for Python because it was easy to read and write it. For great performance, they implemented C++. Python is still considered because of the frameworks it has like Pylons and Django.
- ❖ **Netflix:** Netflix uses Python programming language to help in data analysis from their servers. They also use that in coding and other

Python applications. It uses Python in the Central Alert Gateway and tracking any security history and changes.

- **Dropbox**: This cloud storage system uses Python for the desktop client. Their programs are coded in Python. They use different libraries for Windows and Mac. And the reason being it is not preinstalled on any Mac or Windows and the Python version differs.
- **Reddit**: Python programming language was used to implement Reddit. They choose Python because it has different versions of code libraries, and it was flexible to develop it.

What can you do with Python Programming?

There are numerous applications for Python programming, like machine learning, data science, and web development. In addition, other several projects can use Python skills:

- With Python programming, you are able to automate boring stuff; this is the best approach for beginners. It helps with spreadsheet updates and renaming files. When you get to master Python basics, then this is the best point to start with. With the information, you will be able to create dictionaries, web scraping, creating objects, and working on files.
- Python will help you stay on top of the prices that are set on Bitcoin. Bitcoin and cryptocurrency have become a popular investment; this is because of its price fluctuation. In order to know the right move in regards to Bitcoin, you will need to be alert on their prices. With Python, it is possible to create a price notification for Bitcoin. This is the best way to start on crypto and Python.
- When your intention and plan is to create a calculator, the Python is the best programming language. You will be able to build back-end and front-end services, which

are the best when it comes to deployment. It is important to create applications that users can easily use. If your interest is in UX and UI design, then Python has a graphical user interface that is easy to work with.

- ❖ Python is the best programming language to use when mining data from Twitter. With the influx of technology and the internet, it is easy to get data and information easily. Data analytics is a very important concept; it involves what people are talking about and their behavioral patterns. To get all the answers, Twitter is the best place to start with when your interest is in data analysis. There is a data-mining project on Twitter, and that is when your Python skills will come handy.

- ❖ You will have the ability to create a Microblog with a flask. In recent times, most people have a blog. But again, it is not a bad idea to have your personal hub online. With Instagram and Twitter, microblogging has become a popular concept. With Python skills, you will be able to create your own microblog. When you are into web development, you do not need to be worried about knowing Flask. You can learn about it online and then move to Django which helps in web applications on a large scale.

- ❖ With Python skills, it is possible to build a Blockchain. The main reason for the development of blockchain was financial technology, even though it is spreading to other industries. As of now, blockchains can be used for any type of transaction, like medical records or real estate. When you get to build one for yourself, you will understand it better. You need to remember that, blockchain is not just for the individuals who are interested in crypto. When you build one, you will have a creative way for technology implementation to your own interest.

- ❖ You can bottle your Twitter feed with your Python skills, and this will help in web applications. You can create a simple web app that can help in navigation on your Twitter feed. You will not be using Flask, but rather Bottle; a low-dependency approach that is easy and quick to implement.

❖ There are PyGames that are easy to play with Python skills. You can use the skills to code several games and puzzles. With the Pygame library, it is easier to create your own games and developing it. It is an open and free source with computer graphics and sound libraries, and it helps in adding up interactive functions in the application. There are different games that can be used for library creation.

❖ With Python, it is possible to create something in relation to storytelling. Since the language is easy to use, that is why it creates a better environment for development and interaction.

Importance of Python Programming in the Economics

Most people ask if it is important for economists to learn any programming language. The answer is that it is important since they will use the skills to test and crush data sets. Most of the economist use Python as their main programming language to help with efficiency in order to run complex models. The idea of data analysis is used by other professionals not only by data scientists. Economists learn how to code in order to enjoy the ability to handle bigger data software. Large data can now be handled in spreadsheets when you use the new systems and all that can be done in a shorter time. That is the main reason why economists are adapting to the Python programming language.

Big data is what is used by different people all over. It helps in coding and for market and business intelligence. More spectrums of solutions are created by tech individuals, and they are not just for data scientists. This is why many economists are using and learning programming languages. Economists have been adapting to Python at a slower rate since they did not mostly depend on the data as compared to data scientists. They have adapted to the programming languages because of its flexibility, the breadth of functionalities, development, speed in computing, and the ability to operate between different systems.

Economists will deal with data that is on both low and high frequency. This is because of the increase in digitization and computing. The modern economy brings about greater power in computing and data sources. Years back, coding was used for only back office works, unlike recent times when it is used for front functions, and that is the reason why the use of Python has increased.

Importance of Python Programming at the Workplace

Several benefits come with learning Python if you have not learned the language. There is no need to panic because Python is a program that is easy to learn and can be used to learn other programming languages.

You will understand the importance of Python since it is adopted by different companies like Instagram, Disney, Nokia, IBM, Pinterest, and Google. When you learn about Python, you will have the skills needed to succeed and make good money at it.

- ❖ Python programming language helps in developing prototypes, and the reason is that it is quick to learn and work with.
- ❖ Most of the data mining and automation rely on Python. The reason being that language is better for general tasks.
- ❖ With Python, you will get a better and productive environment for coding, unlike what most programming languages like Java and C++ will do. Most coders claim that with Python, they are better organized and productive when it comes to their work.
- ❖ Since Python is not complicated and any beginner can easily read, learn, and understand, this means that anyone can work with the programming language. All that you

will need is patience and practice to excel with the language. Python helps most programmers and development in large-scale dimensions.

- ❖ Django is an open-source used in web development and application that is powered by Python. With Python, it is easier in improving the maintenance and readability of codes. Python helps in securing coding with updates and maintenance. The reason being it helps in developing quality in the software application. You will also be able to demonstrate all the concepts when using syntax rules. The quality that Python offers in terms of maintenance and readability makes it the best programming language. You can even use English keywords instead of punctuations.
- ❖ Python helps with multiple paradigms that help a programmer know what is relevant in the work environment and requirement. Since Python supports different paradigms in programming, it is capable to feature different concepts that relate to functional

programming. With Python, it is possible to develop a software application that is complicated and large.

❖ Python help in integrating with different operating systems and interpreting different codes. There is a possibility to redevelop this application without recompiling.

❖ Python is able to provide better results as compared to the other programming language because of its library that is robust and big. From the library, it is possible to select the best as per the requirements and add more functionality to that. The feature will prevent having any additional code writing.

❖ Python helps in simplifying any complicated software. This programming language helps in data analytics and visualization in any program that is developing. When you are familiar with Python, you get to complete complex solutions without putting in a lot of time.

How can you earn using Python Programming?

- ❖ **Blogging**: Python programming helps in creating a blog, and the blog is used in making money. There are different types of blogging. You can specialize in programming as your niche in blogging. There are numerous ways to use your blog as a programmer. This includes online coding, charging your premium content, and affiliate links. Ensure all your content is SEO friendly with the relevant keywords that are what is used in ranking your page. In addition, SEO optimization should be on both on and off-page. You will be guaranteed of traffic to the site.
- ❖ **Apps Development**: Your programming skills will be beneficial when you develop an app and monetize it. This programming helps in attaining that. Ensure that you market your app, and use the automatic coding apps that will help in creating the app in a few minutes.

With a great marketing technique, you will be able to make money out of app development. In order to sell it, you need to launch it on the App store.

- ❖ **Freelancing**: This is a situation whereby you offer your services online. You should ensure that you look for the available online platforms and what works for you. You will be able to work from your own work schedule and make money while doing that. Some of the genuine and known platforms include Guru, Freelancer, and Upwork. You can also pitch directly to clients and offer your programming services.

- ❖ You can earn using your Python skills when you make a plugin. The other alternative is having a theme on Wordpress. The best way to do it is by developing many apps and smaller modules like themes and WordPress plugins. This is a great way to make money coding online. Most websites use Wordpress, so if you can create WordPress plugins, you are assured of making a lot of money.

❖ Another way is to be an online educator and start selling your online courses. All this is possible when you use your Python skills and do coding. Most people are adopting online courses where people who cannot attend classes can still learn. When you have a personal website, you can offer free courses and tutorials and have traffic. You can teach many students in economics and finance on how to code and Python skills.

❖ When you join coding competitions, you will be using your Python skills and still earn some good money. You can do development, data science, and design. When you are a winner, you are paid and get access to big companies who are on the lookout for competent coders.

❖ Your Python skills will help in website creation. You can share your programming tips and then display what you have. Ensure that your website shows all your skills, your bans, and your portfolio as a coder. When you have your brand established, you will get more clients that will be willing to get your services and consultation, and you can charge for that. A website can bring your earnings through Google Adsense, affiliate marketing, and sponsored ads.

Chapter 2: Python Programming Concepts

Basic Concepts in Python Programming

The first step to learning Python programming is to make sure that you have understood the ways of learning the language. By understanding how to learn is the most critical skills needed in computer programming. The importance of knowing how to learn is that languages evolve, new libraries are created, and tools upgraded. You must be able to keep up with the changes to be successful in the programming world.

In the modern world, one of the most used languages is Python. This is not just a language, and it is a method of how to do things in a simple and the right way. It is a common high-level language used in open-source. Python is a vast language, and the more you learn about Python, the more information you will need to learn. This is an ironic statement, but that's how it is. Python uses a simple object-oriented approach and high-level data structures. Pythons also use simple dynamic typing and syntax.

Python is a language that is compact, fast, and can efficiently work in any operating system. In addition, if research, you will notice that most of the sites run on Python such as YouTube and Google. Pyramid and Django are frameworks that support Python exclusively, same as the micro-framework like Flask and Bottle, which also supports Python.

Python programming is mostly made up of English language keywords. You will master Python if you can learn the keywords. It will need some practice, and you need to familiarize yourself with the basic concepts before you begin. So, let's start by going through some of them:

- ❖ Properties

Python is dynamically typed, and there is no need to state the variables. The variable is case sensitive; the types are enforced. For example, VAR and var are identified as two separate variables. To find out how any of the objects work, type the following command:

help(object)

Also, dir(object) to find all the methods of a certain option and use object.__doc__ to know the document string.

- ❖ Data types

The next concept is data types. Lists, dictionaries, and tuples are data structures in Python. There are sets of libraries that are available in all versions of Python. Lists are the same as the one-dimensional array, and there can be lists of other different lists. The associative arrays, such as Dictionaries, while the one-dimensional arrays are the Tuples. Python arrays are any type, and its always zero. A negative number starts from the end to the beginning.

- ❖ Functions

The keyword 'def' is used to declare functions. Mandatory and optional arguments are simultaneously set in the function through assigning default values. An argument is assigned a value, and the functions can be returned to the tuple, which can effectively return values using the tuple unpacking. Connecting an object to a variable will remove an older one and also replace the immutable type.

There is a lot of information on Python programming. As always, the main aim is to learn to program, mostly Python. Keep on experimenting and practicing programming to gain the skills and experience. It has a massive array of libraries and functions that you learn and taps into. There are great books and online resources to learn in-depth about Python programming, from error handling, subsets, and classes. You will encounter syntax errors galore, however, keep moving ahead, and you can join the fantastic Python communities and various resources, and you will master it in no time.

The Terms used in Python Programming

As it is the case for any skill, before going full-fledged into practicing the mode, it's important to learn the basic terms that are used in that domain. To better understand your domain, you should learn the terms. For a beginner in Python Programming, we bring a few essential terms that you can be your learning 101 guides.

Below goes the programming terminology for beginners:

- ❖ Algorithm

A set of rules that are created to solve an exact error. Tan error can be complex, such as converting video files to a different format or simply such as adding two numbers.

❖ Program

This is an organized collection of instructions that performs a specific function when executed. It is processed by the CPU, an acronym for the central processing unit of the computer, before executed. Microsoft Word is an example of a program that enables users to create and edit documents. Also, the browsers used are programs that are created to help users to browse the internet.

❖ API

API is an acronym for Application Programming Interfaces. Sets of rules and procedures of building software applications. The APIs help with communication with third party programs, which is used to build different software. Major companies like Facebook and Twitter frequently use APIs to assist the developers to easily gain access to their services.

❖ Bytecode

Python combines the source code into bytecode, an internal presentation of the Python program in a CPython interpreter. Basically, the bytecode is an intermediate language running a virtual machine. The virtual machine is converted into machine code for it to execute it; however, the one-byte can not run on a different virtual machine.

❖ Bug

A bud is a term used to refer to an unexpected error in hardware or software, which causes it not to function. Bugs are often regarded as small computer glitches; however, bugs are life-threatening conditions and causing substantial financial losses. That's why it is important to focus on the process of finding bugs before programs in the applications, and this process is called testing.

- ❖ Code

This is a term used to describe a written set of rules that are written using protocols of different languages like Python or Java. And also an informal use of the code describing text that is written in a specific language, and the reference code can be made for different languages such as CCS Code or HTML Code.

- ❖ Command-line interface

This is a user interface that is based on the text, and it is used in viewing and managing computer files. The interface is also referred to as the command-line user, character user, and console users. In the early 60s, 70s, and 80s, the primary means of interaction with computers on terminals was the command-line interface.

❖ Compilation

Creating an executable program by writing the code in a compiled programming language is known as compilation. With compiling, the computer understands the program and runs it without using the programming software that was used to create it. The compiler translates the computer programs that were written using numbers and letters to a machine language program. C++ is an example of a compiler.

❖ Constants

This is also referred to as Const is a term that describes a value that doesn't change through the execution of the program as opposed to a variable. Constant is fixed and cannot be changed; it can be a string, number, or character.

❖ Data Types

This is a group of a particular type of data. A computer cannot differentiate between a name or a number as a human, so it uses a special internal code to know the difference in the types of data it receives and how to process it. There are various data types, which include character, which is the alphabets, the boolean values are the TRUE or FALSE, the integer is the numbers, and the floating-point number is the decimal numbers.

❖ Array

The array is a list of a grouped type of data values, and the values have the same data type; however, they are different by the positioning in the array. For example, the age of students in a class is an array because they are all numbers, and also, the student's names in a class are array because of its a character data type.

❖ Declaration

This is a statement describing a variable, function, or other identifiers. It helps the compiler to identify the word, understand its meaning, and how to continue the process. They are essential, however, optional and are useful depending on the type of programming language.

❖ Exception

The unexpected and special condition that is encountered during the execution of a program. This is also an error or a condition that changes the program to a different path. For example, when a program loads a file from the disk but the file does not exist. In order to avoid any fatal error, the highly important to handle and eradicate the exceptions in the program code.

Coroutine

A subroutine enters one point and exits in another point while a coroutine is generalized meaning; it enters, exits, and also resumes at many different points. A coroutine is implemented with the async def statement.

❖ Generic Function

Multiple functions are implementing a similar operation for different types. A dispatch algorithm will decide on which implementation to be used during a call.

❖ Python Expression

A piece of code that is evaluated to a value. It's a collection of expression elements such as function calls, names, operators, and literals. An if-statement is not an assignment or an expression because it doesn't return a value.

❖ Python Decorator

A function that returning another function. It joins functionality without modifying it.

❖ Loop

It is a series of instructions repeating a similar process that continues until a condition is completed, and it receives a command to stop. Then a question is asked on the program, and an answer will command the program to act, and then the loop continues to achieve a similar task. The process continues until there is no required action, and the code proceeds on. Loops are one of the most straightforward and powerful concepts in programming.

How to start Python Programming for Data Analysis

❖ Learn Python Fundamentals

We all start from somewhere. The first step is learning the Python programming basics then learn an introduction to data analysis. One of the essential tools to use to start early in your journey is Jupyter Notebook, which is packaged with Python libraries to assist you in learning both Python programming and data analysis.

❖ Practice Mini Python Projects

With hands-on learning, you will be surprised how soon you will be ready to take on small Python projects. For example, tying things likes calculators for an online game or trying a program that gathers the weather from Google in a particular city. By doing mini projects like these will enable you to learn Python. Such programming projects are the standard for all languages and the perfect way to better understand the basics. Start by building your experience with APIs and begin web scraping. Python will help you learn to program while learning web scarping will assist you in gathering data.

❖ Learn Python Data Science Libraries

Unlike other programming languages, in Python, there is the best way to do something. The best and essential Python libraries for data analysis are Matplotlib, Pandas, and Numpy. For data visualization, use the Matplotlib library. For exploring and playing with data, Pandas and Numpy are the best library to use.

❖ Build a Data Science Portfolio as you Learn Python

Building a portfolio is essential for an aspiring data analysis. The projects should be various datasets, and the portfolio doesn't need to have a specific theme. Find a dataset that you have interest in and find a plan of putting all of them together. Displaying such projects help with future employers, and it shows that you took the time to learn Python and other essential programming skills.

❖ Apply Advanced-Data Analysis Techniques

Focus on sharpening your skills, and your data analysis journey will be full of constant learning; however, there are advanced courses to help you cover all the bases. And be comfortable with classification and regression. Also, step into machine learning and using scikit-learn to create neural networks. In addition, programming projects involves creating models using live data feeds.

How to Install Python

Python is a common programming language for application development. Python design focuses on code readability and clear programming for both small and big projects. You are able to run modules and full application from a massive library of resources on the server. Python works on various operating systems, such as Windows. Installing Python on the Windows server is a straightforward process of downloading the installer, and running it on your server and configuring some adjustments can Python easier.

To begin working with Python, you will first need permission from the Python interpreter. There are different ways of achieving these:

- ❖ Python is available from the website Python.org. Download the right installer for your operating system and run it on the computer.

- ❖ Linux provides a packaging manager that you can use to run your install Python.
- ❖ The macOS uses a package manager called Homebrew to install Python.
- ❖ iOS and Android are mobile operating systems, and you will need to install apps that will support Python programming. And this is the best way to practice your coding skills at any time.

And the other way is by finding websites that provide the users the opportunity to get into Python interpreter online, and there is no need to install it on their computer. And also a chance that the Python will be preinstalled in your operating system. If that's the case, then the version might be outdated, and you need to get the latest version.

In this chapter, you will learn the process of setting up the Python on macOS, iOS, Windows, and Linux. Let's begin!

❖ Windows

Python does not come preinstalled in the Windows systems. However, installing Python is a straightforward process. All you need to do is to download Python installer on the website, Python.org, and then run the program.

Here is how you install it on Windows:

❖ *Downloading Python installer*

➢ Opening your browser, get into the Python.org website, and move to the download page for Windows.

➢ Click on the heading "Python release for Windows and click on the link.

➢ Scroll down and select Windows 64-bit or 32-bit Windows.

When using Windows, you either download a 64 or a 32-bit. The difference between these two is,

➢ Use a 32-bit installer if you have a 32-bit processor.
➢ If you have a 64-bit system, then both of the versions will work on both of the purposes. Using a 32-bit will require less memory; however, using a 64-bit will work best with applications of intensive computation.
➢ When you are not sure of which version to install, choose a 64-bit version.

Additionally, when you install the incorrect version, and you wish to change it and choose another version, you may do that by uninstalling Python and re-installing it by getting the version from Python.org.

❖ Running the installer

When you chose and downloaded the installer, then double-click the downloaded file and run it. You will see a dialog box that has a prompting button instructing you to run the installation. Don't forget to click the box that indicates "Adding Python to PATH"; this will confirm that the interpreter is added in the execution path. The final step is to click 'Install now,' and this is all the required steps. After a few moments, a working Python will be installed on the system.

❖ Windows Subsystem for Linux

When your computer has Windows 10 Creators installed, you have a different way of installing Python. A feature called Windows Subsystem for Linux is used in this version, and you can run the Linux environment straight into Windows without having to use the virtual machine. After you have installed the type of Linux distribution you require, go ahead and install Python from the console window. A similar way can be done if you are natively using a Linux distribution.

- ❖ Linux

Most Linux distribution comes with preinstalled Python; however, it might not be the latest version. To be able to know what version you have, there is a process you can do to find out. Open a prompt window and then try the following commands below:

Python version.

Python2 version.

Python3 version.

The version of the commands from the three commands will answer with the version. If it is not the latest version, you will install the newest version. The procedure of this depends on the Linux distribution running on your computer. It's much useful to use

Pyenv, a tool used for multiple Python version management on Linux.

- ❖ Ubuntu

There are different versions of the Ubuntu distribution, and the installations are different. Identify your Ubuntu versions by trying these commands:

$lsb release a

No-LSB module available

Distributors ID: Ubuntu

Descriptions: Ubuntu-16.04.4.

Release-16.04.

Code name-xenial.

Ubuntu versions 16.10 and 17.04 don't have the Python 3.6, as it's the universal repository.

❖ Linux Mint

Both Ubuntu and Mint use similar packaging management systems, making life much easier. Installation instruction for Ubuntu can also be used in Mint. A deadsnakes PPA working well with Mint.

❖ Debian

Some evidence shows Ubuntu's 16.10 method can also work for Debian, however, there is no path for it to work on Debian 9. But you can make Python from the following source.

One disadvantage of Debian is, it doesn't install Sudo commands by default. Before installing Debian, you are required to check a compiled source from the Python instruction:

$-su.

$apt-get-install sudo

$-vi /etc/sudo

Then use sudo vim commands or any preferred text editor to open /etc/sudoers file. Adding the following text line at the end and changing "your_username" with the real usernames:

your_usernameALL=(ALL)ALL

- ❖ Open SUSE

There are various websites which outline ways of getting zypper to add the newest Python; however, they might be outdated. They don't successfully work, and it's best to build Python from the source. Begin by installing the development tool that is completed in YaST through the menu or the zypper.

$sudu zypper install-tpatterndevel_C_C++

The procedure will take some time, and it involves installing 154 packages; however, when completed, you will be able to build the source.

❖ Arch Linux

It's fairly strict to keep up with the Python release. Arch Linux might be preinstalled, and if it is, it is not the newest version, use the following command:

$packman -S Python

Chapter 3: Python Programming Lessons

How to Learn about Python Programming

The first thing you should know before learning Python is that this is not going to be easy. This should not scare you at all because I think there is a really good way to make all these a little friendlier. Many beginner tutorial videos talk of how Python programming language gets complicated with time and how the long run is not going to be so much exciting. Well, it really depends on what really fascinates you into the Python world.

Let us venture into some of the features and thoughts that an individual is highly expected to dive into in the first place.

- ❖ Think of what dived you into considering Python language.

It is super easy and fun to learn something if there is a grand reason behind all that. Frankly, Python language learning needs massive motivation so as to grasp every good detail, and therefore, your objective of learning should be your motivation so as to eventually evade boredom. Pick a field area that you are interested in and one that you are so ready to put your massive efforts into. Multiple kinds of fields are available, for instance, games, mobile development, websites, and many more that actually call for good knowledge and skills in Python programming language. Getting motivated to acquire all these so as to specialize in your desired field area should definitely be the main key to learning and getting advanced in the Python language world. You sure got this.

❖ Master the basic syntax.

Apparently, the basic syntax is the most important factor in your Python world foundation. Concentrate deep on the basic syntax and get to master how the structure behaves and the various operations involved. However, it is advisable that you do not really need to spend much time in this because you actually get to master the basic syntax as you try to implement them in the various projects that you may consider to start with. This will also provide an opportunity for the novice to learn from the possible mistakes that are likely to be committed when coding with Python language.

❖ Involving multiple structural works.

Learning and implementing out the new things learned has always been the best way of learning in history. Well, get the basic part of the Python language basics and try to implement the concept learned in various projects that use Python language. As discussed, this will help the learner to identify the faults that are likely to be committed during programming, learn from every error and get really advanced in working with Python projects and coming up with viable projects that are pretty good in solving human problems.

❖ Build something.

Structural work will definitely get you into great curiosity and fascinated by what you can actually build and get it to be productive. This is definitely a good strategy that will get you into a bigger position in the Python world. What is more amazing is that you will not be implementing what has been learned but also get to grasp so many new concepts and ideas as you get along in your learning journey. Always try to commit to some various projects by yourself and get to know how far you can go and also where to rectify in your learning journey so as to become an amazing expert in the Python programming world.

Start with the basic kind of projects as you try to get advanced with time where you will be dealing with the tough kind ones that you be amazed at how simpler they may sometimes get a thing that you totally did not expect.

- ❖ Collaborative measures.

It is highly recommended that, as a learner, you ought to surround yourself with peers who are also learning the same language as you. Well, two heads are actually better than one, and every individual normally has different views and angles that he or she comprehends a certain concept. Go and exchange ideas and work on multiple projects once in a while and see how far you can go as a team and see the scope of new things and new ideas that you are capable of grasping. Learning as a community creates that positive attitude and the willingness and passion to learn more gets to increase with time.

❖ Open-source.

Fortunately, many companies normally publish various open sources on the internet of multiple software that they are working on. This should give the learner the opportunity to get involved in certain pull requests, an activity that will developers get to view your code and see what you have been working on. This may even land you your first job at any of the desired software companies and eventually get to grow as a person. Furthermore, contributing to various source codes on the internet will also enhance your communication with multiple developers around the world, and you eventually get to grow in your career and also as a person.

❖ Make coding a habit.

Mastering and grasping the basics in Python programming language calls for good consistency and great motivation for success to follow your way. Spare around 30 minutes of your time every single day as you commence your learning journey and see coding becoming your habit, especially if you are totally new to the programming world. The start is always the hard part but I believe with the amount of full energy that one entails at the starting point will definitely pass you through the successful journey in this Python language world. All the best.

Where can you learn about Python Programming?

There exist multiple and several learning sources that an interested programmer can venture into and grasp the wide knowledge and skills of the Python programming language. For instance:

- ❖ **Websites**
- ❖ Cybrary

The website entails various Python programming courses for beginners who have a huge interest in the Cybersecurity field. The courses are super helpful and get you started towards your end goal journey.

- ❖ Sololearn

This is another amazing site full of several programming languages in wide knowledge, good structural examples, projects, challenges, and many other helpful tasks. Sololearn normally tutors from the basic steps to the complex and advanced steps with so many tips and assistance that will eventually get you through the end goal.

- ❖ Code academy

Code academy is another online site that is contented with basic, intermediate, and advanced levels of various programming languages. A beginner can, therefore, expect to find practical and much detailed contents of Python programming language that will clearly create a huge impact in his or her technological world.

- ❖ EDX

This is also a good learning site that just calls for signup and getting started with your new account where you will learn good Python learning skills and knowledge and eventually get the chance to acquire a certificate that is pretty much valid and one that will eventually get you to your first Python income-generating project.

- ❖ GitHub

GitHub is common in most developers as a source of learning and getting advanced in various programming languages through the wide use of open sources. Developers are likely to get engaged in various pull requests and get to collaborate with various kinds of Python developers from all over the world on various viable projects. This will not only give the developers the opportunity to learn new concepts about Python language but also enhance appropriate communication between developers.

- ❖ Stack overflow

Stack overflow is basically an online platform where developers get to inquire about anything, discuss a certain topic, get answers for their unknown questions in mind, and basically get to learn anything in which they highly desire to learn. A developer interested to grasp a certain complicated topic on Python language can inquire, and he or she will surely get much assistance.

- ❖ YouTube

YouTube has become a famous type of social media that is pretty much used for learning purposes. This is because it is much practical and structural as depicted by its most online learning videos. Most companies like Edureka have their accounts on YouTube where people are obligated to subscribe so as to follow up on their learning videos and also be informed on the Python language day to day updates.

❖ Python books.

Books are famous in learning because they are much detailed and easier for reference purposes when trying to master a new programming language. Python books are available in the local libraries around your vicinity, local book stores, and even online via the Amazon site. Some of the most loved Python books include:

- ❖ Headfirst Python by Paul Burry - This book is highly recommended to the novice who is pretty much interested in grasping the basics of the Python language. The book entails illustrations and so much great assistance that a beginner would call for when getting into the Python programming world.

- ❖ Python crash course by Eric Matthes – The book immerses an individual into several hands-on projects that he or she is expected to venture into as part of the learning journey. He or she is expected to learn the basic fundamentals of the Python programming language, and eventually becoming an accomplished beginner once the book is completed. Some of the fundamentals of the Python language entail popular Python web frameworks that are super important in web development.
- ❖ Python programming by John Zelle – The book is designed for the computer science students who have the intention of grasping the basic idea of Python programming language for the purpose of their academic achievement.

❖ PDF and other texts.

The internet entails various kinds of PDFs that a learner can consider to opt-in and learn various concepts and the basic facts in Python programming. There exist various PDFs for the beginners and also the intermediate kind of learners where they are likely to get exposed to the good Python programming concepts and the basic facts and achieve the very best out of all these in the endpoint.

❖ Social media communities.

With the wide use of social media, it is so much easier for learners to learn together via various online sites like Whatsapp group, Telegram channels, Facebook communities, and so much more. Through these sites, developers are able to discuss the clear Python language concepts that appear to be much complicated to some people and even undertake various challenges together. Learning Python programming language through various tech communities has been confirmed to be so much helpful.

What is the Cost of Getting a Python Certification?

The cost of acquiring a Python certificate is getting gradually getting expensive with years. In recent times, acquiring a Python certificate at the moment can cost around 290$ to 350$ in most of the popular learning institutions like the Python institute. The amount of finances includes full examination fees that a programmer is required to go through before getting a valid Python certificate. Acquiring a Python certificate can land you to a brand new job if you are a new developer in the programming industry, and on the other hand, get you promoted to a much better position in your firm. I wish you all the best in Python studying and achieving your deserved certificate

The Best Python Course

As learners, we ought to commit ourselves to the best king of Python courses so as to grasp the best in all that, and eventually, come up with something really viable to the universe. Below are some of the best courses that a learner is pretty much expected to dive into and extract success from them:

❖ The numpy stack in Python

Identified as deep learning prerequisites course outline, this kind of course particularly targets programmers who are interested in data science and machine learning using the Python language. The programmer is likely to explore into several kinds of Python libraries, for instance, numpy, pandas, and scipy that will establish a perfect base for the programmer in deep machine learning, data science, and even artificial intelligence. The programmer is also likely to get exposed to the various advantages and the cons of utilizing certain Python libraries in their projects as they work on multiple data science and machine learning projects.

❖ Python core and advanced kind.

First, this course is totally free, and therefore, financial disabilities should definitely not be the reason as to why a particular programmer should not venture into this course. The course is much detailed describing how Python should be installed, illustrating how a programmer is expected to execute his or her first program, Python command line, Python constructs, object-oriented programming with Python, Python libraries, Python libraries, and so much other Python basics that are super important.

❖ Python 3.0 boot camp for novice programmers.

If boot camp courses for Python programming language excites you, then this is the right side for you. Okay, I have good news; the course is totally free, and you are, therefore, not going to spend even a single dime from your savings. This is a simple, detailed, and particular kind of Python 3 programming course and the programmer is, in the end, expected to learn the basic concepts and working illustrations of the Python 3 programming language. The course is suitable for both those with no prior knowledge of Python programming and also advanced programmers.

❖ Learn Python programming in just 100 steps.

This is the perfect course for a programmer to learn the Python 3 basic steps and get a clear comprehension of what is actually is entailed. The course was founded a great and popular Udemy instructor and blogger from Udemy who outlines the basic Python programming concepts coupled up with the respective tools and integrated development environment that is constituted in the Python programming world. The programmer will also get the opportunity to venture into various hands-on exercises of different topics in Python like data structures, object-oriented programming, handling various kinds of Python errors, and in the end, get to work on various kinds of projects that will definitely turn out to be pretty much successful.

What Job can you get with Python?

Python language is widely used by large tonnes of companies in our current world. Some of the companies include Instagram, Reddit, Google, Spotify, Netflix, and even in our favorite local banks. Let us dive into some of the income-generating projects that are as a result of implementing Python language:

- ❖ A Python developer.

This career is best suited for a developer who is pretty much contented with Python language at a much wider scope, and he or she is well advanced with the programming language. A Python developer is involved in tasks like building and developing various websites, optimizing data algorithms, implementing various security measures and protecting data, solving multiple problems in data analytics, and also writing reusable and efficient kinds of codes. Well, being a developer exposes a developer to various income-generating tasks that can make eventually him or her land into good jobs in major startups in the world.

❖ Data Analysts

Most companies are looking for individuals with the ability to play with a large number of numbers using Python libraries like the scipy and pandas that are normally implemented in large data sets. An example of a company that is in great search of data analysts using Python is Bloomberg.

❖ A product manager.

A product manager basically talks to the users of a certain product directly and gets to grasp some important data from them concerning the product in question. Through this, they are able to derive new features for their products, spot the possible market gaps, improve on their current tools or acquire new tools for their products, and so much more. This is so exciting, right? Companies like Snapchat is hunting for such great individuals.

❖ Financial advisers.

Bank financial advisers are highly advanced in the Python programming language where they are able to master the behavior of people's bank accounts in form of several sets of data and various bank operations, hence provide guidance services to various customers who happen to be in need.

❖ Software engineering.

Software engineers are involved in analyzing the user's needs and designing, testing, and evaluating applications for the purpose of satisfying the users as part of the end goal. Software developers are happily paid large chunks of money, and they also get the opportunity to get exposed to greater career opportunities.

❖ Research analysts.

Research analysts are normally involved in researching, analyzing, and coming up with viable reports concerning a certain product in the market. They are able to succeed in this in-depth market research by implementing various Python libraries to the available sets of data of the products.

❖ Machine learning engineers.

Machine learning engineers normally develop multiple machines, software, and other computer systems that are highly capable of learning and implementing any kind of knowledge that has been comprehended and excluding the use of set instructions. This is what individuals advanced in a

Python programming language can do with the kind of knowledge they have in their minds.

❖ Quality assurance engineer.

These kinds of engineers are able to track the development process of a product from the commencing point to the endpoint using various Python libraries and methods. Quality assurance engineers are super famous in the technology industry, and they are paid a good amount of money that is worth getting the right skills and knowledge using Python programming language and other various techniques.

❖ Web developer.

Python is a great part of website development through its various frameworks that offer a great part of website development. Some of the common frameworks of the Python language include Django and the pyramid that are used by most website developers.

❖ Game developers.

With knowledge in Python libraries like the pygame and panda3D, a developer gets to acquire the skills and knowledge that is pretty much needed in developing various games. Game developers earn an average amount of salary that is still a goof financial figure.

Chapter 4: Operating Systems

What's your definition of an operating system? An operating system is a type of system software which allows users to run their application programs on their computing devices. Your computing devices ought to have an operating system that assists in the managing of your hardware resources and also provides services to your application programs. Python language, like any other programming language, also runs on various operating systems of your machines. The are various operating systems that support Python which include Linux, OS X, and also Windows. In this chapter, you shall learn on the various mentioned operating systems and also be aware of the different ways of Python troubleshooting.

Python on Linux

Linux is some sort of a Unix operating system that operates under the open-source license. An open-source operating system means that you can do some modification on the system software, and you can even distribute the modified version to others. Its ability to be performed some modification makes it so popular and preferred to, unlike the other operating systems. Linux operating system is supported by many devices such as mobile devices, computers and also servers.

How is this operating system used?

Almost all versions of this operating system provide user interfaces to users and manage their hardware resources. Moreover, web servers such as Apache utilize the Linux operating system as compared to other operating systems.

The different versions that exist for the Linux operating system are referred to as the distributions.

These distributions can be downloaded online with no cost, saved on your USB drives, and installed on your preferred machines. The Linux distributions that exist include the following:

- ❖ Linux mint
- ❖ Debian
- ❖ Ubuntu
- ❖ Solus
- ❖ Fedora
- ❖ Opensuse
- ❖ Manjaro

Some of the Linux distributions are tailored for servers, desktops, and many other systems. The most commonly used Linux distributions for desktop are Ubuntu server and CentOS, which are free with no cost but do not offer support for their users. Contrarily, the distributions that offer support for their users but are costly include Red Hat distribution and SUSE Enterprise. This operating system is a secure and robust system, and hence there is no need for the users to install any antivirus software on their machines.

Which versions of Python can be run on Linux distributions?

Different versions of the Python language can be run on different Linux distributions. The most commonly used versions are Python version 2 and version 3. You are, however, mostly advised to use version 3 as compared to version 2, since it is actively maintained. The two versions have different syntax so you need to decide on only one version to use on your computing device.

How to use Python on your Linux distribution.

You can use Python on Linux using the Integrated Development Environment (IDLE). It is a graphical user interface that allows its users to write Python code on it. To use Python on your Linux distribution, you need to also install packages that are compatible with your distribution.

Some individuals prefer using the command line version to the IDLE versions. Ubuntu distribution normally comes with a command-line version already pre-installed which makes your work easier. You can decide to choose the version that you are comfortable with. Furthermore, most of the Ubuntu tools support Python as compared to other distributions.

At most times, a novice who uses a Linux operating system, normally run their first Python scripts on a command-line version before using Python text editors. With time, they get familiarized with the text editors and other programs known as interpreters. An interpreter is a program that converts the lines of codes written by a Python programmer in a way that a computer can easily understand. It enhances the programming, and the computers are able to process and execute the lines of code.

Python programming

When using the command-line interface, right-click on your desktop and type in Python on the Linux terminal. Still, at the command prompt, you can type in "Hello world", and the text that is written will be displayed on the next line. This can be hectic sometimes, so many Python programmers decide to switch to using the Integrated Development Environment instead.

To get started with the IDLE on Linux operating system, you need to open a terminal window on your machine and type "idle", of course, without the quotes. After a while, a graphical shell will load. To be provided with some sort of text editor, click on the file, then click on a new window to begin writing a Python script. Try writing some lines of code on the text editor. Save your file with a .py extension and try running it by clicking on run then run a module from the menu. Above is all the information you need to know to get started with Python on a Linux operating system.

Python on OS X

You are lucky if you are an OS X user since most of your machines come when Python is already installed on them. For those who do not know if Python is installed on your machine, you can open a terminal and type Python –version. You should make plans for downloading a set up of Python if you do not have any from your machine. The few ways of installing Python on your OS X machine include the following:

❖ From the source

This method involves installing Python from the source code. Most programmers prefer this method with the desire of doing some customization on the binaries during the building process.

❖ From packaged binaries

You can get the Python binaries from the Python website which assists you in making upgrades on your Python versions. You need to make sure that the Python version you want to download matches the type of your CPU architecture. The types are either 32 bits or 64 bits.

❖ Homebrew

This is the package manager for OS X. It enables its users to install, uninstall, and even make updates on their packages using the command line. It works the same as the **apt-get** that is available on Ubuntu distribution on Linux machines. It makes work easier for OS X users.

You need to install the latest Python version with the new features.

All Python programmers need a powerful development tool known as a text editor that assists them in their code execution and testing of their lines of code. Different Python programmers have different tastes of text editors. The default Python text editor for this operating system is the TextEdit which unfortunately does not support all the formatting options. You need to select another text editor great for you. There are, however, few Python text editors for the OS X operating system. Below is a list of the most preferred text editors to use on your OS X machine:

- ❖ IDLE.

This is the common and the simplest text editor most individuals use to get started with Python. It comes bundled together with Python set up during installation, and it's located in the application folder. It enables its users to perform modifications on their lines of code and also get to see the code results.

Python programming

Let us now get started on how to launch IDLE on your OS X since most novice Python programmers use this text editor when beginning off with Python.

- ❖ Type in and click on the terminal on the search button located at the top right of your screen.
- ❖ A blank terminal window will load after a while.
- ❖ Type in "idle" on the terminal, and of course, without the quotes. Then press return.
- ❖ IDLE will start up definitely then get started with your Python programming.

Since this text editor does not have advanced features as compared to the other text editors, you can choose another text editor when you get familiarized with Python coding after some while.

- ➢ PyCharm.

This is the most popular Python text editor on an OS X operating system. It offers both the free and paid versions to its users. PyCharm was developed by Czech company Jetbrains back on 3rd February 2010. It makes work easier for its users by providing the necessary tools for analyzing their lines of code, debug on them, and also test on them. Most web developers use PyCharm when working with Django which is a Python open-source framework.

The three editions for PyCharm include the following:

> ➢ PyCharm Edu.

PyCharm Edu is a free edition that provides the necessary tools for professional development. You do not need to worry if you do not have experience with it, it comes with every tool build in it necessary for learning.

It has its bases on the IntelliJ platform enabling it to provide smart and productive features of code inspection, visual debugging, and also code completion.

➢ PyCharm Community.

This is also a free PyCharm edition. PyCharm Community comes along with an intelligent editor, a graphical debugger for your codes, a test runner, tools for inspecting your code, and also for navigation. It is more advanced as compared to the PyCharm Edu. PyCharm Community has, however, fewer features than the PyCharm Professional, as you shall see on the next subtopic.

➢ PyCharm Professional.

This is the most advanced edition of PyCharm. PyCharm Professional is paid for, unlike the other editions. It possesses all the features available on the PyCharm Community Edition. Most scientific and web developers utilize in this edition. It offers support for a number of frameworks such as Jupyter, Django, and Flask, and even Database and SQL.

The extra support that this edition offers that are not available on PyCharm Community includes scientific tools, tools for website development, Python profiler, and also tools for Database and SQL management.

After installing on the edition of your choice, you can get started with new projects using this text editor. You need to click on "create new project" on your screen, and your new project will pop up.

- ➢ Eclipse.

To use Eclipse as a Python IDE, you need to install it together with the PyDev plugin. PyDev is a free and open-source plugin that allows programmers to enjoy the features of Eclipse while writing Python lines of code. It has the features of:

- ❖ Analyzing and completing code.
- ❖ Refactoring.
- ❖ Code debugging.
- ❖ Providing hints while typing.

- ❖ Integration with Django, Jython, Pylint, Unittest and even IronPython.
- ➢ Gedit.

This is a general-purpose Python text editor for the GNOME environment. It is simple and easy to use as compared to other text editors. You can get started with Gedit on your OS X operating system by going through the following steps:

- ❖ Launch on your terminal by hitting on the command button plus the space button. Type the word terminal followed by hitting on the enter button.
- ❖ The next step is to install brew on your computing device using some commands from their website.
- ❖ The last thing to do is to type in the following command on your terminal **brew install gedit**

The productive features that gedit offers for its users include the following:

- ❖ Remote file editing

- ❖ File reverting
- ❖ Support for print and print preview
- ❖ Support for the clipboard commands (cut, copy and paste)
- ❖ Wrapping of text
- ❖ The numbering of lines
- ❖ Highlighting the current line
- ❖ Matching of brackets
- ❖ Fonts and color configuration
- ❖ A complete user manual which is available online
- ❖ Backing up of files
- ❖ Undo features

➢ TextWrangler

TextWrangler is a free text editor that can be used on any machine using the OS X operating system. It's a mini version of BBedit which has all the required features as BBedit. You can download this text editor online to get started with the TextWrangler text editor.

After installation, go to the right top of your screen, specifically on the search button and type in TextWrangler. You can create your first program by typing in print "My first program". You should then save the file with a .py extension, as it is normally done for all Python files. TextWrangler will display some color effects on your line of code which helps most Python programmers be aware of the syntax errors so as to work on them very easily.

TextWrangler has the following features for its users:

- ❖ Navigation of functions
- ❖ Feature of coloring the syntax of the lines of code
- ❖ Support for opening and saving text files suited on remote FTP servers
- ❖ Support for multiple clipboards
- ❖ Undo features

➢ Sublime Text

Dany Log

This is a free text editor most users using OS X operating system prefer to use. It offers the best performance since it has a powerful Python API. You can look for a sublime text download setup online and install it on your computing device. Launch the text editor by double-clicking on the file **Sublime Text** which comes with a .dmg extension. You are then required to drag the **Sublime Text 2.app** into the applications folder. Then get rid of the **Sublime Text.dmg** into the thrash. The text editor is then ready for use.

The amazing and beneficial features offered by Sublime Text include the following:

- ❖ Users can perform multiple customizations on the editor, unlike other text editors. You can edit on the menus, snippets, and macros.
- ❖ It allows users to perform selection on multiple lines of code. This enables faster manipulation of the files.
- ❖ It is able to recognize the type of file.

- ❖ It highlights the syntax used in the lines of code.
- ❖ Automatic indention.
- ❖ It offers connectivity with the VSCs (Version Control Systems) such as Git.

Now that you are aware of the different tools of Python development, you can get started with Python on your machine with an OS X operating system.

Python on Windows

Windows operating system does not have a system to support the installation of Python on machines. Therefore, Python is made available to Windows users through the use of MSI packages. These packages have a release for a couple of years that come along with an interpreter and libraries for its users. There are also a number of different installers Windows users can use to get started with Python.

➢ The full installer.

It contains all kinds of components needed by any Python programmer working on any kind of project.

➢ The embeddable package.

This is a minimal Python environment in a zip file that is normally contained in a larger application and thus not directly used by the end-users.

➢ The Microsoft package.

This is the simplest installer Windows users can use when starting off with Python. It provides suitability to execute Python packages and scripts and also provides commands for the Python launching and its tools. It mostly performs better on a Windows 10 operating system. Most students use this package when installing Python on their Windows machines.

This package is free at no cost; you need to select the right package from the Microsoft store. After installing it, you can launch Python from the Windows start button or the command prompt by typing in **Python.**

To make any kind of uninstallation, you can go back to the Windows start button, type in **Python,** right-click on it, and press on uninstall. All packages acquired during installation will be removed but the virtual environments will still remain.

➢ The nugget.org packages.

This is a minimal Python installer on Windows. It promotes the building of the Python packages and scripts execution. Its downside is that you cannot make updates on it and has tools for user interface integrated with it.

Let us now dig deeper into the various steps of getting Python installed on your Windows machine.

❖ Open your browser and go to the official Python website.

- ❖ Navigate through the download page on the Windows section.
- ❖ Hit on the link with the latest Python version.
- ❖ Scroll down the page and click on the setup with the CPU architecture that aligns with your machine which is either 64-bit or 32-bit.
- ❖ Once the download is complete, double-click on the file.
- ❖ Then hit on the **install now** section. Your installation is now complete and ready for use.

Python Troubleshooting

Encountering problems with Python on your operating system is a common thing for all beginners in Python. Most of the problems arise due to cramming of syntax leading to errors and bugs. This section will outline some of the common problems and also provide you with different ways of handling them.

➢ Syntax errors.

This type of error can be detected before running on your program. They mostly involve typing errors that do not follow the rules of the Python language, thereby affecting the structure of your lines of code. Syntax errors may arise due to the following reasons:

- ❖ Failing to indicate the colons
- ❖ Failing to insert brackets
- ❖ Misplacing a keyword
- ❖ Wrong indentation
- ❖ Missing out a keyword

A solution to this problem is to run several lines of code after a while so as you are to rectify the issue as early as possible.

➢ Runtime errors.

These are errors that arise when your program executes. Most of the Python runtime errors are caused by the following:

- ❖ Calling on invalid functions
- ❖ Using variables on your Python code before defining them
- ❖ Failure to indicate quotes on function names
- ❖ Dividing variables by zero
- ❖ Making access to files or lists which do not exist

➢ Semantic errors.

This is also referred to as the logical type of error. These are errors associated with the design of your lines of code. They do not indicate that you have an error like the above-mentioned errors. They execute your lines of code incorrectly and give out the wrong output.

They, in short, do not perform their execution as expected. Semantic errors are the toughest type of errors to handle for most of the Python programmers since programmers are forced to go back to their whole lines of code and try to find for the source of error.

Below are some of the causes that lead to the rise of logical errors.

- ❖ Writing wrong names for the variables
- ❖ Making mistakes on the Boolean values
- ❖ Wrong precedence of the operators
- ❖ Wrong indentation. Mostly contributed when you copy-paste multiple lines of codes

You should avoid too much copying of the huge blocks of codes.

Chapter 5: List

What is a List?

Python has a total of six sequences built into it with the list being the most common one moreover. This data structure is changeable (mutable). This means that once you create it, you have the ability to change it. Lists in Python are said to be the same as arrays which are used in other various languages such as c++ programming. Having a standardized list format is not always the case, but when studying or actively developing with Python, you find that lists are what you put to use a lot. A list in Python may or may not contain a variety of data types. These data types include integers, strings, and objects. A Python list is helpful when implementing a stack or a queue.

Putting a Python list to use:

•A Python list is a very helpful tool when it comes to protecting your data sequence and iterating the same data sequence.

•A list is executed as a value putting commas to separate between the square bracketing.

•A list in Python is, at all times, ordered and has a given count. The list is indexed starting from zero (0)and the elements follow an indexing scheme depending on the classification.

•A Python list is an example of a container in the structure of data, and they are used to hold numerous amounts of data.

•This Python List stores data elements in a sequential way.

•A Python list is made up of two types of data combination namely heterogeneous or homogeneous.

- A list in Python is the same as the C++ and the C arrays in their respective programming languages.

- When working with many values that are related, a list is the best structure to implement since it enables the collection of data that belong together and keeps it at one reference point. This helps you reduce the size of your code, and the implementation of operation carries the same effect on multiple values at a go.

For the purpose of this beginners guide, let's write a simple list :

#Flying_birds

flying_birds = ['Vulture', 'Swan', 'Crane', 'Goose', 'Mallard', 'Stork']

When we hit the print button, we expect our output to look exactly as the list created:

print(flying_birds)

Output

['Vulture', 'Swan', 'Crane', 'Goose', 'Mallard', 'Stork']

The above elements are in a sequence that is well ordered, and an individual element in the list can be called through indexing.

Indexing of a List

Every item belonging to a list corresponds to an index numerical value, which is an integer starting from 0 as I mentioned above.

For our list flying_birds, the indexing is as follows:

'Vulture'	'Swan'	'Crane'	'Goose'	'Mallard'	'Stork'
0	1	2	3	4	5

From the above items, the first item 'vulture' takes the position of index zero (0), and the list comes to an end at index 5 which is 'stork'.

In Python, each item comes with a specific index number attached to it. This means we can call a specific item individually through its index syntax enabling us to manipulate it as we wish without affecting other items. This is also the same way other sequential data types function.

We can now call an item discretely by referring to its specific index number :

#Flying_birds

Print(flying_birds [2])

Output

Crane

The indexing of the above data is arranged as shown below. You can call a specific item through its index numbers as shown:

Flying_birds[0] = 'Vulture'

Flying_birds[1] = 'Swan'

Flying_birds[2] = 'crane'

Flying_birds[3] = 'Goose'

Flying_birds[4] = 'Mallad'

Flying_birds[5] = 'Stork'

In the event that in flying_birds, we list an index of a number that is more than five(5), the outcome will declare that the item is out of range, and it is not valid.

Print(flying_birds [22])

Output

Index error: the list index is out of range

Apart from applying a positive number index, we are able to get access to items from a list through negative number indexing, but the twist is counting is done backward from the last time in the list, unlike the positive number indexing where counting starts from the first item on the list. In negative indexing, the index number starts at -1. This method of indexing comes in handy when we want to pinpoint a particular item that falls at the end of a given long list.

From our same list on flying_birds, the negative indexing looks like this:

'Vulture'	'Swan'	'Crane'	'Goose'	'Mallard'	'Stork'
-6	-5	-4	-3	-2	-1

Therefore, when you want to print an item by the name 'Mallad' when using the negative index numbering, it should be like this:

Print(flying_bird[-2])

Output

Mallard

Since you have the basic information on how to write a list and how to call a specific item from a list, I will show you how to link a string to a specific item using the plus(+) operator. For this example, our string will be: 'Birds can fly high especially the', and we will use 'Crane' which has an index number of [-4]. Let's do this:

#Flying_birds

Print(' Birds can fly high especially the ' + flying_birds[-4])

Output

Birds can fly high especially the Crane

NB: We were able to concatenate the item at index [-4] with the string ' Birds can fly high especially the '. The plus(+) operator can also be used to link together two or more lists.

How to Change Elements

With Python, you can alter the contents of your list as per your needs.

This is made possible by the indexing of items on a list. By changing the string value of an item at a given index, you can affect what the system prints.

On our list 'flying_birds', we want to change the item at the index position 2 from 'Crane' to 'Alpine Chough'. We do it like this:

#Flying_birds

Flying_birds[2] = 'Alpine Chough'

When we print 'flying_birds', we expect it to read differently:

Print(flying_birds)

Output

['Vulture', 'Swan', 'Alpine Chough', 'Goose', 'Mallard', 'Stork']

This type of change can also be applied to a value in a list by using the negative indexing instead:

Flying_birds[-4] = 'Alpine Chough'

Print(flying_birds)

Output

['Vulture', 'Swan', 'Alpine Chough', 'Goose', 'Mallard', 'Stork']

The results of the negative indexing are the same as those from the positive indexing.

Since this data structure is mutable, it enables us to make changes on a list, especially to a specific part without having to re-write the whole list again, saving us time and allowing updates to be made easily.

How to Remove Element

At this segment, I want to show you how to remove an item from an existing list. Elements in a list are removed using the 'delete' statement. This statement will delete a value at a specified index number.

From our 'flying_birds' list, we want to remove the item 'Goose'. In our list, this item is positioned at index number three(3).To remove this item, we will use the **del** function statement then move on to call the variable list and the index numbering of the item:

#Flying_birds

flying_birds = ['Vulture', 'Swan', 'Alpine Chough', 'Goose', 'Mallard', 'Stork']

del flying_birds[3]

print(flying_birds)

output

['Vulture', 'Swan', 'Alpine Chough', 'Mallard', 'Stork']

After printing the item at index position 3, the string 'Goose' does not appear in our list of flying_birds.

When you have a long list and you want to delete multiple strings, you don't have to delete them at a step-by-step process. You can specify the range and add the delete statement. Say you want to remove not only the item 'Goose' but also 'Mallad' and 'Storks'. We will use the range as shown below :

#Flying_birds

Del flying_birds[3:5]

Print(flying_birds)

Output

['Vulture', 'Swan', 'Alpine Chough']

Apart from the delete statement, you can also use the remove () method to do away with any element in a Python list. The statement functions in a way that when its called, it assumes that the string in the syntax is unwanted and aims to remove it from the list.

In the event that an element is passed to the remove statement and doesn't exist, the system on printing displays a ValueError.

The return() only removes elements from the list; it does not add elements to an existing list.

Example

#Flying_birds List

Flying_birds = ['Vulture', 'Swan', 'Alpine Chough', 'Mallard', 'Stork']

the 'swan' elwment is removed

Flying_birds.remove('swan')

#Update flying_birds list

Print('Update list :',flying_birds)

Output

['Vulture', 'Alpine Chough', 'Mallard', 'Stork']

In the event that a list has multiple elements, we can remove them; but the remove element() only removes the first instance example:

#Flying_birds

Flying_birds = ['Vulture', 'Swan', 'Swan', 'Swan' , 'Alpine Chough', 'Mallard', 'Stork']

Remove the swan element

Flying_birds.remove ('swan')

#Update flying_birds list

Print('Update flying_birds list:',flying_birds)

Output

['Vulture', 'Swan', 'Swan' , 'Alpine Chough', 'Mallard', 'Stork']

Here, only the first 'sawn' is removed.

Trying to delete an element that does not exist results in the following error:

Traceback (the last call) :

File "…………" line 6 in <module>

Flying_birds.remove ('ostrich')

ValueError: list.remove(6) element at index 6 is not on the list.

This error messaged is displayed because the element Ostrich is not on the list.

Apart from the two methods, you can also use the pop () statement to specifically specify an element that you want to delete.

How to Add Elements

Adding elements in the Python list can be made possible by using append (), insert (), and extend () methods. Let us now get deeper details of the above-mentioned methods.

Append ().

This method is used to add an item at a finishing end of a current list. It does not produce a new list but rather does modification on the already existing list. The syntax normally used for the method is the **list. append (item).** Append () adds items to a list of strings, numbers, and even objects.

Below is a procedure of how to insert an element by applying the method under discussion. There is an example provided below that uses **fruit** as the name of the list.

fruit = ['mango', 'orange', 'banana', 'apple']

This is how you will do it when you want to add another item on the list using append ().

fruit. append ("watermelon")

The **output** will be:

['mango', 'orange', 'banana', 'apple', 'watermelon']

In situations where you want to add another list of objects as a parameter using the append () method, this is how you are going to do it.

fruit.append (["pear", "guava", "avocado"])

The **output** will be:

['mango', 'orange', banana', 'apple', 'watermelon', ['pears', 'guavas', 'avocado']]

In a situation where you want to append two arrays using the numpy module, this is how you are going to do it.

In our example, the arrays to be used are:

array1= [2]

array2= [1, 5, 7]

You first need to import the module as **np** then follow the steps below.

array1= np. array([2])

array2= np. array ([1, 5, 7])

result= np. append (array1, array2)

print ('result: ', result)

Output

result: [2, 1, 5, 7]

Extend ().

This method is used to add elements of one list into another list. Its syntax is **list.extend (list 1)**. Extend () merges simply merges two lists. Below is an example that you can take a keen look at.

list1= ['cookies', 'biscuits', 'juice', 'sweets']

list2= ['cake', 'yogurt', 'soda', 'crisps']

When you want to add the elements of list2 to list1, this is how you will do it.

list1.extend (['cake', 'yogurt', 'soda', 'crisps'])

The output will be:

['cookies', 'biscuits', 'juice', 'sweets', 'cake', 'yogurt', 'soda', 'crisps']

Insert ().

This method requires an index and the value to be inserted. Check out the example provided below.

myExample= ['love', 'Python', 'programming']

The element to be inserted at index 0 of the list is I.

These are the detailed steps you need to follow.

myExample.insert (0, "I")

print myExample

Output= ['I', 'love', 'Python', 'programming']

How to Organize a List

Sorting your list when practicing Python can be tough sometimes, right? Do not have any worries because this section is going to guide you on every kind of steps necessary. Python uses the list. sort () method that enables you to organize your list in different ways such as in:

- ❖ Ascending order.
- ❖ Descending order.

You can also use a built-in method sorted () that generates a sorted list from any iterable. Most of the Python beginners have issues when deciding on which method to implement during the list organization. You are advised to mostly use the list. sort () method because of various reasons:

- ❖ List.sort () method is much faster than the other method. It loads the list first followed by the method that calls the function without any arguments as compared to the sorted () method that calls the functions using the list as the arguments.
- ❖ List.sort () method works with the list in place, and therefore, does not have to make a copy of the list. Contrarily, the sorted () method has to make copies of the list and works with any iterable. This makes a list. sort () method more efficient.

However, both the list. sort () method and sorted () methods organize the lists in ascending by default. This section guides you on the various ways of how to organize your Python lists. It will tackle lists containing numbers, strings, tuples, and also objects.

- ❖ Numbers.

Sorting numerical in Python is a walk in the park. The list containing numerical in Python is the simple one to organize. Below is an example provided on how to organize your numerical list. L will be used to represent the name of the list.

Ascending order

L=[67, 3, 16, 74, 2]

L.sort()

print (L)

Output=[2, 3, 16, 67, 74]

Descending order.

L=[67, 3, 16, 74, 2]

L.sort (reverse=True)

print (L)

Output=[74, 67, 16, 3, 2]

If you want to implement on the sorted () method, here is how to do it:

Ascending order.

L=[67, 3, 16, 74, 2]

sorted_list= **sorted** (L)

L

[67, 3, 16, 74, 2]

sorted_list

Output= [2, 3, 16, 67, 74]

Sorted () method does not require definition since it is a built-in function found on every installed Python.

It does not contain any additional arguments because it is organizing the values in L from the smallest to the largest.

This method does not change the original values of L in place.

- ❖ Strings.

A string is a set of characters. In a scenario where you are provided with strings and not numerical, here is a guide on how to do your organization using both of the two methods.

Let's say you are provided with a list **F**.

Ascending order

F= ["guava", "mango", "pineapple", "avocado"]

F. **sort** ()

F

Output= ['avocado', 'guava', 'mango', 'pineapple']

Descending order using sorted () method.

F=["guava", "mango", "pineapple", "avocado"]

sorted (F, reverse=True)

Output= ['pineapple', 'mango', 'guava', 'avocado']

In a different scenario where your list of strings is composed of both uppercase and lowercase strings, the output will differ from the rest mentioned above. Uppercase strings in Python are normally treated as lower characters than the lowercase strings. Here is an example that will help you understand better.

Let's say you have a list R, below will be the output.

Ascending order.

R=["town", "country", "Kenya", "home"]

R. **sort** ()

R

Output= ['Kenya', 'country', 'home', 'town']

Case insensitive lists can be sorted through the use of a certain parameter referred to as **key** which is utilized by both the sort and the sorted method. It assists in specifying the function to be called from the items in a list. Take a keen look at the example below.

R=["town", "country", "Kenya", "home"]

R. **sort** (key=str.lower)

R

Output= ['country', 'home', 'Kenya', 'town']

The str.lower has instructed the sort method to perform the sorting on all the lowercase strings. The parameter has enabled you to define the customized function.

- ❖ Tuples.

When it comes to tuples, the first element is the one under comparison that makes it similar to how strings are done. Both of the sorting methods can be used when organizing lists in tuples. Take a look at the example given below.

sorted ([(5, 4), (3, 3), (4, 8)])

Output= [(3, 3), (4, 8), (5, 4)]

However, this might not be the case in all situations. Some scenarios might have a tuple whose first element indicates a name while the second element indicates the age of an individual. Such situations will force you to implement the **key** parameter again so as to organize the tuple by age.

You will customize the sorting by defining the key function. You can achieve that by doing the following:

#define the custom sort for your list

#return the numerical value of the tuple

L=[("Eva", 21), ("John", 53), ("Mary", 14), ("Reddington", 45)]

#call on the function

#run the L list

print (L)

#The result will be

[('Mary', 14), ('Eva', 21), ('Reddington', 45), ('John', 53)]

- ❖ Objects.

This is the final type of list in Python you are going to learn in this section. In a situation where you are handling objects, you can organize them using the **key** parameter. Let's say you have a **Person** class with attributes of **name** and **age**, this is how you can organize it in Python.

class **Person:**

#Define the variables used

def _init_ (self, name, age)

#Declare the variable name

#Declare the variable age

self. age= age

Try creating objects of the class **Person** and insert them to a list **L**. This is how it can be done.

Mary= Person ('Mary', 14)

John=Person ('John', 53)

Eva= Person ('Eva', 21)

Reddington= Person ('Reddington', 45)

L= [Eva, John, Mary, Reddington]

You can organize the objects of the class by using the attributes that you prefer.

When you make up your mind to use its **name** attribute, this is how it is done.

#assign the key parameter used to a lambda

#run the names of the items in the list

#The result of the code will be:

Output= ['Eva', 'John', 'Mary', 'Reddington']

This is how it is done when you decide to organize the objects by the **age** attribute.

#assign the key parameter to a lambda

#print the names of the elements according to the attribute

#The result of the code will be:

Output= ['Mary', 'Eva', 'Reddington', 'John']

Custom sort definition on any object in Python is a piece of cake. Good luck with that.

Chapter 6: Variable and Simple Data Types

Dictionaries

Dictionaries are data types in the Python programming language that is much similar to a list of certain objects contained in a particular collection. Let us venture into some of the similar characteristics and differences that lists and dictionaries share, so as to get the basic idea of what dictionaries are all about. Similar characteristics of these two data types include: They are both mutable, hence due to any shifting at any particular moment of time, they are dynamic. They are able to change in a way that they are to grow and shrink during any episodes and a dictionary is capable of containing another dictionary in it, and a list is too able to contain another list in it hence concluding that these data types can be nested. The only difference between these two data types comes from how the data values are accessed. Lists are normally accessed by various indexing operations whereas dictionaries are basically accessed by the use of various kinds of keys.

Dictionaries basically consist of some key-value pairs that normally are the key to a specified associated value. We define a dictionary in Python by first enclosing the entire list using curly brackets, placing a full colon that separates the key pairs to the associated value placed, and lastly by using a comma mark in separating the various kinds of key pairs that are available in the dictionary. Another way in which dictionaries can be constructed in the Python world is through the use of dict() function in the program. This one works in a way that the value of the argument in the dict() function consists of the keys and the respective values that have been paired along with it.

Kindly remember that square brackets are normally used to contain the key-value pairs in the program in question. Once dictionaries have been defined, it is possible to display its contents where they get displayed just the same way they were defined in a structural manner.

Dictionaries are accessed by specifying its relevant key inside square brackets symbol, and in a case where a certain key does not exist in a particular dictionary, an exception is raised right away as an error made. It is then possible to add a certain entry in a particular dictionary where a new key with its value is assigned in the program. In updating a particular entry, a new value is just assigned to an existing key. During the delete of an entry operation, a del statement is normally used specifying the actual key to delete.

Lastly, methods and various operations are normally implemented in dictionaries so various tasks can be achieved. For example, if a developer has the intention of copying a particular dictionary, he or she is obligated to use the copy() method of the Python programming language.

Some of the other methods include:

- ❖ Clear method - this method clears all the kinds of elements that are present in the dictionary.
- ❖ Get method - this one gives the value of the key that has been specified in the dictionary.
- ❖ From keys - this kind of method gives out a particular amount of keys and values from the dictionary.
- ❖ Keys - outputs a list that entails the keys in the dictionary.
- ❖ Pop - this method removes the elements with the specified keys.
- ❖ Value method – this method gives out a collection of all the values that are present in a certain dictionary.

Functions

A function is defined as a set of various statements that takes in some inputs, computation is then carried out, and output is eventually produced at the end. The purpose of the functions is to evade writing the same set of code all over again during different cases, and instead, just call the function in the program. A function in the Python programming language is created using the def keyword and a certain name which is then followed by the parenthesis and full colon symbols. Calling a function that normally happens at the program consists of the function name that is then followed by the parenthesis symbols. Information is then passed to various functions in the form of parameters that are placed in parenthesis after the function name. Multiple parameters can be placed in the brackets and then separated by the use of commas inside the parenthesis.

In the Python language world, there exist different kinds of parameters that are commonly implemented by a number of Python developers. Default parameters are the kind of parameters that can be defined as a parameter that normally assumes a default value if at all no value has been placed in the function call for that particular argument. There are also keyword arguments which allow a developer to specify a particular argument name with values in a bid for the caller to ignore the order of the parameters in question. To add, there is also the variable-length arguments that normally sums up the normal and keyword variable number of arguments in a particular program that has been coded using the Python programming language.

Looking at the types of functions, there is an anonymous function which is a type of function that does not bear any kind of name and the one that uses the lambda keyword instead.

Classes

A class is basically a code of template that is used in creating various kinds of objects or entirely a major blueprint that is used in creating objects in the Python programming language. Classes consist of member variables with several kinds of methods involved and any other operations that may be involved in the program. A class is constructed by including the keyword class just before the desired class name.

Classes in the Python world normally bear a certain function called init function that normally executes when a particular class is being initiated and where values are being assigned to key-value object properties. This function is usually called automatically every time the class is used to create an object in a particular class. Another term, methods, basically defines the functions that belong to specific objects in the program, and when defining particular methods, you usually provide the first argument to the method using a self keyword. Methods are normally able to access the class attributes in the program.

Testing your Code

In a Python programming language, there are several technique methods that are used in testing a particular kind of code. Let us venture into the actual methods that are normally involved:

❖ Automated versus manual testing.

Exploratory testing is a type of manual testing that is committed without a specific plan, where a developer is just trying to explore the actual application. In a bid to complete certain amounts of manual tests, a developer is obligated to draft a list of all the available features that a certain application contains, the various kinds of inputs that are normally accepted, and the possible expected results. With this, the developer is expected to go back to his or her list whenever changes are made to a particular set of programs, an activity that is so much tiresome and unsatisfying. It is at this point where automated testing comes in.

Automated testing is the execution of the set program of code by a script in place of a particular human. Python language comes in handy is a set of tools and certain libraries that aids a particular developer in making automated testing to its application.

❖ Unit tests versus integration tests.

A unit test is basically a kind of smaller test that checks whether a single component in a particular program works the right way so as to make it functional, whereas an integration test is the type of testing that ensures all the components that are involved in a particular set of program work well with each other. Both unit tests and integration tests can be written in a specific program.

Test runners are basically tools that pick up the source code directory of a particular kind of program that contains unit tests and various settings, gets to execute them, and eventually outputs the results to the log files or the console.

Let us look at some of the common test runners that are used by programmers:

- ❖ Pytest

This particular test runner supports the execution of various unit cases. Good example of the great characteristics used in pytest test runner include: supports the use of the built-in assert statement instead of using the special self assert method, offers support for filtering various test cases, it has the ability to rerun from the last test that had failed, and establishes a favorable ecosystem of hundreds of plugins with the intention of extending the functionality.

- ❖ Unittest.

Unittest is available in the Python standard library since the 2.1 version and can probably be seen in the commercial Python applications and various open-source projects. It contains both a test framework and a test runner. To add, a few requirements are called for when using unittest during testing of your particular program. You are required to put your tests into classes as methods, and one is also expected to use special assertion methods in the particular unittest, for instance, using test case class in place of the built-in the assert statement.

In order for this particular operation to work, one is required to import unittest from the particular standard library, then create a class called test sum that gets to inherit from the test case class, change the test functions into methods by including self as part of the first argument, then change the assertions to use self asset equal method on the particular test case class, and eventually change the entry point of the command line to call unittest main.

❖ Nose or nose2

If you are a novice in using test runners, it is highly recommended that you commence with nose2 in place of the nose when running various kinds of your programs. Nose or nose2 is compatible with multiple unittest frameworks and can be used in place of the unittest test runner for its functions okay. To commence with the nose2 test runner, install the nose2 test runner from pypl and execute it from the command line. The test runner will try to discover all the test scripts named test py and the various test cases that are inherited from the unittest.

File and Exceptions

For file handling operations, Python language treats files as either text or binary, a concept that is so important to most of the programmers and where every line of code that is available composes of a set of characters that eventually form a particular text file.

Every line in a file is normally terminated with the presence of special kinds of characters commonly known as the end of line characters like a comma and a new line character. It normally finalizes the current line and then notifies the computer interpreter that a new line has begun. Users are able to handle various kinds of files where they are able to read and write codes, explore the various file handling options as part of the operations that are normally involved in files.

Let us look at some of the operations that are normally involved in the reading and write files:

- ❖ The open function.

This type of function in the Python programming language normally opens a file in the read and write mode. The open function goes along with just two kinds of arguments, the actual file name and the specific mode, that is whether to read or write. There exist three kinds of modes: reading which is represented by r, w symbol for writing value for appending, and r plus for both reading and writing mode. The mode argument is not usually mandatory, and if not placed in any program, the default mode is normally r for reading mode. Looking at the modes:

- ❖ The read mode - in a case where you need to derive a string that entails a string of characters in the file, we utilize the file.read() operation. Alternatively, the programmer can decide to call a specific amount of characters which will then be outputted as a string, and in the exact number that was argument-ed, that is file.read(3) operation.
- ❖ The write mode - the file.write() operation is normally used. For instance, file.write("This is the writing program") that enables you to add up the contents of the particular program.
- ❖ The append mode - This one is capable of enhancing clean kind of syntax and exceptions when getting to work with various kinds of codes.

- ❖ Write a function with the function

Write function can also be used with function to write some content to a particular set of programs.

- ❖ Split function.

Programmers are capable of splitting lines using file handling in the Python programming language. This is capable of splitting the variable when any space is encountered, and we may also split any kind of character as per our own desire.

This and many more other functions are normally involved in file handling operations in the Python programming world.

Exceptions are the events that normally occur during the execution of a particular program that disrupts the normal path of various instructions of a particular program. This is basically an object in a Python programming language which normally represents a certain error that has been involved in the program.

An exception that has been involved in a program should be handled quickly unless the execution gets to be terminated.

Exceptions can be handled in a way that a programmer can place his or her set of code blocks after a set of the keyword try and a set of full colon symbols prior to it and an except statement after the set of blocks of code. The except statement is then followed by a set of blocks of code that is able to handle the situation in the program the right way.

A few points to take during the above operation are that a single statement can bear several except statements which are super useful when the try block is capable of giving out different kinds of exceptions, a generic except clause can be provided so as to handle various kinds of exceptions. An except clause can also be included where the set of code gets to be executed only when the set of code in the try block does not raise any kind of exception, and the else statement is definitely a good zone for a particular kind of program that does not require any kind of exception to be involved.

Exceptions can also bear arguments that normally give an extra piece of information about a certain problem in question. The contents of the argument vary with each other according to the kind of exception involved, and the variables received can either be single or composed of multiple values that are in the form of tuples. The argument is normally optional; when no argument has been placed in the program, the exception argument becomes none.

Exceptions are raised in various ways using the raise statement as follows: the raise statement, followed by exception, argument, and then the traceback.

The argument at the final and the traceback are usually optional, and if they happen to be present, that becomes the traceback object that gets to be used for the exception. To add, there exist user-defined kind of exception which allow the programmer to create their own exceptions by deriving classes from the standard built-in exceptions that have been used in the program.

User Input and while Loops

A while loop in the Python world is basically used to iterate a particular set of code as long as the specific condition being tested gets to remain true. The body of the program only gets to be executed only if the test condition set gets to remain true and the execution takes place over and over again until the test expression set evaluates to false that will eventually terminate the program. Any non zero that is interpreted is termed as true, whereas the none and zero values are normally interpreted as false.

When while loop with else is used, the else part of the program is normally executed only if the set condition in the while statement is termed to be false. In a case where a break statement gets to be used after the while statement piece of code, the set of code in the else statement gets ignored by the interpreter. Therefore, it can be concluded that when else statement only gets to be executed when the set condition in the while statement is termed to be false and when no break statement has been included after a while set of code statements.

For the user inputs, there are two functions that a programmer can initiate so as to get various kinds of inputs from the user and where the results obtained can be stored into a particular variable in the program.

The raw input function used in the Python programming language is used to read various kinds of strings inputted by the users. For instance, name= raw_input("What is your name?"). On the other hand, the input function can just be able to read integers. For example, age= input("what is your age?")

Exception handling of inputs always ensures that the user has entered some valid kind of information into the program database. One of the ways of ensuring correctness and the accuracy of the information that gets to be inputted by the user is avoiding any kind of errors that may be involved in a particular program. For example, using the while loop command in your particular set of program that has been used which will be executed in a way that the code will continuously run until a valid integer has been inputted by the user in question. Except statements can also be used in the particular program as part of raising an exception, an event that will curb many applications from crashing from time to time, and instead of second printing out of the output gets to be enhanced.

Chapter 7: Data Visualization

How to Generate Data

Data visualization consists of various tools for generating data. The tools used in the generation of visualized data in Python include the following:

- ❖ Cluvio.

Ever wished for a tool that can enable the creation of exciting visualizations? Cluvio might be the tool that you have been looking for. Cluvio is a company based in Germany that was founded in 2016. It offers exciting and amazing features for its users and enables you to execute SQL queries from your database.

More than 100 companies trust this tool of data visualization due to various reasons:

- ❖ Amazing usability and design. Cluvio has a great design for its users that is of good quality and a simple interface for the novice Python programmers to understand. The design has high standards that enable the creation of interactive models.
- ❖ Supports the analysis of SQL-based data. It analyzes any structured query language data, generates charts, and shares them out which is not seen on other tools for generating data.
- ❖ Creates interactive boards. Interactive dashboards are mostly preferred by users. Cluvio generates interactive boards that make data visualization exciting for Python beginners.
- ❖ Supports both R language and SQL. Cluvio integrates with both SQL and R languages which makes it a powerful tool. It is able to generate efficient statistical data using the R language that most data engineers use in data visualization. This makes the tool more popular than other tools.

❖ Suitable for both small and large companies. Cluvio consists of different pricing options that favor both the infant companies and the major companies. It has a free pricing option plan, a starter plan, and also a pro plan for the big companies. Each of the plans has different features for its users.

One of the downsides of Cluvio is that it does not support other file formats such as the CSV and the Excel formats.

❖ Google charts.

You have all heard of Google, right? Google offers vast tools for its users across the world that help in the running and execution of data. A Google chart is one of the tools being offered that assist you in your management and in the presentation of data. Google charts represent and generate your data in the form of piecharts and pictographs. This makes it easier for users to read the data and make the analysis. Google charts are free tools that make them popular as compared to other tools that are offered at a fee.

Moreover, Google charts do not require any programming skills for you to use them. It mostly favors the novice Python programmers who do not have adequate programming skills since they are just starting off their programming journey. They are able to generate visualized data from statistical graphs and piecharts.

Google charts also offer the benefit of free virtualization hosting for its users at no cost. This enables the sharing of data across the website. Google charts also enable programmers to generate on their images from charts and other plots by the use of an API (Application Programming Interface) known as the Image Charts API. With this API, you are only required to establish a URL which will contain your information on the data and its formatting. You do not require any type of coding for you to generate an image from a Google chart.

Its main downside is that it has poor support for its customers, unlike other tools of data visualization. Also, there may be possibilities of the loss of your graphics in situations where the Google servers are down. Many of the novice Python programmers suffer this since they forget to back up their graphics. The final downside of a Google chart is that it denies its users the ability to perform some modifications on their code since the code is not quite exposed.

- ❖ Infogram.

This is a tool used to generate data from marketing. It has high capabilities for publishing as compared to the tools mentioned above. Infogram is much popular for its simplicity to use since it contains a user-friendly interface for the novice Python programmers to understand. It also offers great support for customers unlike it is seen on other tools such as the Google charts. Infogram is mostly preferred by the managers and the software engineers involved in the data virtualization.

Inforgames focus on images to be able to generate data. They provide its users with templates that allow customization based on the statistical data and any kind of graphics. It is offered at a fee of approximately $19 per user every month. This makes it unsuitable for not the well-established firms. Its performance is not quite functional as compared to other tools.

- ❖ Visme.

This is a tool used for the design of shared stories in a way of presentations. Visme consists of three pricing plans which include the individual plan, the business plan, and the education plan. Most individuals utilize this tool due to its simple user interface that provides ease of use. Visme also provides vast graphs and resources that assist in the creation of stable and attractive models. It also offers good quality customer support that helps in assisting the novice Python programmers.

The downside involved for this tool include issues with the text boxes and varying quality of the design when files are exported. This makes it hard for beginners to use. Individuals who mostly prefer this tool are the marketing directors and also the persons involved in media productions.

❖ Flare.

This is an Actionscript library that enables users to create any sort of virtualization from the charts to something interactive. Flare enables you to make presentations of the charts in a reasonable manner. Users also have the capability of making customizations on the dashboards by the use of text boxes so as to point out the insights.

The drawback of this tool is that the virtualization made when using this tool is quite unsuitable for mobile applications. It is also tough to integrate this tool with some website applications. Moreso, the flare tool takes time to be updated and it, therefore, produces outdated dashboards not forgetting the many bugs it contains.

How to Download Data

Gone are the times when most of the novice Python programmers experienced hard times when downloading their visualized data. It has been fortunately made easier nowadays to draw your data by implementing a few modules. The modules being talked about here are Pandas and Matplotlib.

Let us now get into details on the various modules that will help you download your Python data.

❖ Pandas.

They are Python packages with numerous tools for analyzing data. Pandas are used for the management and importation of datasets in Python using a variety of formats. They are also integrated with some of the methods that can assist in the data analysis in Python.

Many individuals prefer using pandas in data visualization due to the following reasons:

- ❖ They enable data presentation in a way that can be easily analyzed. They do this via the use of the Series data structure and also DataFrame data structure.
- ❖ Pandas consist of a variety of methods suitable for the efficient filtering of data.
- ❖ They also contain a set of utilities that support the input and output operations. Pandas can read the different formats of data such as CSV and also ms excel.

How can you install pandas?

Pandas do not come with the normal Python distributions. You need to install them on your terminal to use them. This can be done by the use of the pip command that normally comes with the

Python distribution. Run the **pip** command together with pandas on the terminal of your machine.

In situations where you have anaconda already installed on your machine, you can run the **conda** command together with the pandas on your terminal to make the installation successful. You are advised to install the latest version of pandas on your machine. You are now ready to go.

Let us now dig deeper into the two types of data structures mentioned above that are used by pandas in Python.

- ❖ Series.

This type of data structure is the same as a one-dimensional array. A series of data structures provides storage to any type of data, and its values cannot be changed. The first element of the data structure is normally assigned an index value of 0 while the last element is assigned an index of N-1. N represents the total amount of elements in the data structure.

To first establish the Pandas series:

- ❖ You need to import the pandas' package on your terminal.
- ❖ **Series** is then created by using an array after calling on the **pd. Series ()** method.
- ❖ The contents of the Series will finally be displayed after running on the print () command.

The output of the content will consist of two columns, whereby the first column will be the indexes of the elements, while the second column will contain the elements used in the array.

A **series** can also be generated by the use of the numpy array then, later on, made some conversion to a Pandas series. This is how it can be done.

#import on pandas on your terminal.

#import on numpy.

#import on the system command.

#call on the file object for the output to be displayed by the print () method.

#call on the numpy library to create an array of your elements

#assign an array to the Pandas series.

#call on the print method to display the output.

The output will contain a first column with the indexes of the elements, and the second column will be elements of your array.

- ❖ DataFrame.

This type of data structure in pandas is in the form of a table that displays data in the terms of rows and columns. It is a 2-dimensional array, unlike what is seen in the Series data structure. The values of the columns can be modified without affecting their identities.

DataFrame data structures can be generated from scratch, or you can decide to use on the numpy library and convert them later to the data structure.

By building from scratch, you can follow the following steps:

#import pandas on your terminal

#create a DataFrame.

#assign DataFrame to a variable using pandas where you also assign the values of the rows and columns as part of your arguments.

#call on the print method to display the output.

The output will also contain a column of indexes at the start just like you have seen on the Series data structure.

How do you retrieve data using pandas?

Pandas can read data from file formats such as CSV, that consist of values separated by commas. This is made possible by the use of the read_csv method.

You need to do the following to achieve the data importation into the pandas DataFrame.

#import on pandas.

#call on the file with the CSV values using the read_csv method. You need to specify the location of the file using arguments.

#call on the print function to display the values of the file.

In situations where you have large datasets, you can retrieve a few numbers of rows you want to retrieve the data from by using the **head ()** method. Moreover, if you want to retrieve a specific row or column of a large dataset, you can use the **loc ()** method.

Pandas can also read and retrieve data from files with the file formats of ms excel with the use of the **read_excel** method.

- ❖ Matplotlib

Matplotlib is another great visualization library used in Python. It was developed by John Hunter in 2002. It is established on the arrays of NumPy and enables its users to get access to huge amounts of data. Matplotlib is available on Windows, Linux, and also on OS X operating systems.

This Python library is integrated with the plots of lines, bars, and also histograms that normally assist you in the pattern and trends discovery, and you are also able to make correlations of your data.

Below is the detailed information on the different plots used in Matplotlib.

- ❖ Line plot.

To generate this, you will go through the steps below:

#import on the Matplotlib Python library.

#assign values for your x-axis.

#assign values for your y-axis.

#plot your values using pyplot function.

#use the show function to display your plotting.

Your line plots will finally be generated.

- ❖ Bar plot.

The procedure for this is quite similar to that of a line plot. You are required to follow the following steps:

#import on the Matplotlib Python library.

#assign values for your x-axis.

#assign values for your y-axis.

#plot your bar using the pyplot function.

#use the show function to display your bar.

Your bar plot will, at last, be displayed by this Python library.

- ❖ Histogram.

On this plot, you are required to call on the import function of Matplotlib, and then assign values for both the y-axis and the x-axis. Make plotting of your histogram using the pyplot function and then call on the show function to display the histogram.

How to Work with APIs

An Application Programming Interface (API) is a software that acts as an intermediary between two applications and enables them to work together. Let us apply a real-life example for you to understand better. In a situation where you are a customer in a certain restaurant, you need to make an order to the waiter for you to get served with a meal of your choice. Therefore, you will make an alert to the waiter who will take your order to the kitchen team since they have the responsibility of preparing your meal. The meal gets prepared, and the waiter will bring the meal back to you. The waiter in our case scenario is the API while you, as the customer, are the system user, and the kitchen team act as the system you are using. The point is now at home, right?

This section is going to cover the different ways of working with APIs used in data visualization. Some of the APIs used in data visualization include the following:

❖ Bokeh.

This API was established by a development team of Anaconda back in 2012. It is a free API with no cost and was created to visualize the data applications from web browsers. Most individuals prefer using this API because it enables them to establish on their statistical plots, and it also supports data visualization from other Python libraries such as Matplotlib.

Bokeh has three types of levels for different persons who have varying levels of control. The uppermost interface of this API is designed for the creation of simple charts using different methods of histograms, line plots, and also the bar plots. You can acquire the plots by implementing on the numpy arrays and also the DataFrames.

The interface at the middle level enables you to have control of the blocks building the charts. The lowest level is specifically designed for the developers and engineers of software. They normally study every data element of the charts.

❖ Seaborn.

This is a top-level interface that has its bases on the Matplotlib Python library. It promotes the creation of exciting and attractive plots. It is more powerful than the Matplotlib since it can generate a graph with only one line of code unlike when you are using Matplotlib.

Seaborn can be integrated with the DataFrames of pandas, and therefore, be able to produce amazing interfaces. The downside of this API is that you need to be aware of how Matplotlib works to have an easy time when working on the Seaborn API.

❖ Plotly.

Plotly is a stable data visualization API mostly for websites. Are you aware that this API can be accessed from a Python notebook which makes it unique from the rest of the API? It is considered as a special API since it possesses the functionality of 3D charts. Plotly supports many file formats such as CSV and the xls formats. It enables its users to simply make modifications on the graphs. Also, Plotly has great compatibility with many languages such as R and Python and tools like Matlab.

❖ Pygal.

Pygal is quite similar to Plotly and Bokeh. It is mostly used for Python data visualization, but it is also considered to be used in HTML projects. It provides plots with interactions that are normally on the online web browsers. Pygals produce plots as Scalable Vector Graphics (SVG) that are not found on any other data visualization APIs.

It is, however, suitable for small datasets. In situations where you use large datasets, the charts become slow, and they become difficult to process the data.

Pygal also enables the creation of amazing and attractive charts with the use of a few lines of code.

- ❖ Geoplotlib.

Geoplotlib is an API that is mostly concerned with the geographical location and is also involved in the generation of maps. The kind of maps that can be generated when you use this API is the chloropleths and also the dot density maps. You need to install Pyglet on your machine when you decide to utilize Geoplotlib.

This API comes in handy when you do not have adequate tools for maps since most of the standard Python installation does not have tools for maps.

- ❖ Gleam.

This is another amazing data visualization API. It can integrate with any Python library. It provides its users with the ability to switch any analysis to an interactive website application with the use of any scripts of Python programming. You do not require to have any skills of HTML, CSS, and JavaScript to use this API.

This is the reason why most individuals prefer using it.

- ❖ Altair.

This is a simple Python library used in statistics and is established on the Vega and the Vega-Lite. Many individuals prefer it because it is user-friendly that makes them be able to understand well. Its source can be obtained from Github. It supports the creation of attractive data visualizations with only a few lines of code unlike it is seen on other data visualization APIs.

Altair performs better on a Jupyter notebook, and it can be installed on your computer using the **conda** command. The steps involved to create a simple Altair chart include the following:

- ❖ Generate an object for the chart using a DataFrame for Pandas.
- ❖ Select the right marking for your chart.

- ❖ Assign values to the x-axis and the y-axis using the **encode** command with the right number of columns.

- ❖ ggplot.

This is a Python library mostly based on ggplot2 which is an R system. ggplot enables you to come up with plots containing a peak level of grammar. It has tight integration with pandas. Its user interface is simple and exciting to learn from as compared to other APIs which are complex that turn off most novice Python programmers. The charts on ggplot are easy to customize, and they offer elaborate views for you to easily understand. Ggplot also merges multiple datasets into one graph.

ggplot has its downsides that include:

- ❖ Requires more lines of code, unlike other APIs.

❖ Its production results might be at fault since it mainly focuses on establishing attractive graphs with amazing color schemes.

Chapter 8: Web Applications

A web application runs on a remote server as a software application. Most of the time, web browsers are for web applications like the internet. Some of the applications are used for intranets, schools, firms, and organizations. They are not the same as other applications since you do not need to install them. Some of the common web applications include Flickr, Wikipedia, Facebook, and Mibbit. They are popular since most of the operating systems are on the web browser and programmers can change them with ease.

Several benefits come with using web application:

❖ They do not need to be installed since they run inside a browser.

- ❖ They do not require a lot of space for storage only a display of data.
- ❖ With web applications. It helps with compatibility problems; all is needed is a browser.
- ❖ Most of the data used are remotely stored; hence ease of cooperation and communication.
- ❖ Web application helps in mail and communication.

Apart from the listed benefits of web applications, there are also drawbacks:

- ❖ Most of the known web applications will seem to look different as compared to the regular programs. The reason is that they run inside a browser. The user experience might be different and not liked by many.
- ❖ To be able to follow standards, web applications need to be coded, and any small changes will prevent the web application to be used in any browser.

- There is a need to have a connection between the web application and the server in order for it to run smoothly. For the connection to happen, you will need bandwidth. And when the connection is not adequate, you may experience data loss or the application will be usable.
- Most of the web applications depend on the server that hosts them. When it is off, the web application is not usable, but the traditional applications will still work.
- The overall control of the web application is with the mother company. They have the power to create a new version when they feel like it.
- When the data is remotely stored, exporting it to be used by other applications will be hard.
- Web applications enable the company to track all the activities of the users, hence privacy issues.

At this point, you need to know how a web application works. Most of the web applications are coded in a language that is browser supported, like HTML or JavaScript. And the main reason is that the languages depend on the browser in order to execute their programs. You should know that some of these applications are dynamic, and they will require server-side processing. Others are considered static and will not need any processing from the server.

When you have a web application, you will need a webserver to manage all the requests that the client has. The server will help in performing all the tasks and store data and information. The application server includes ASP, PHP, and JSP. A normal web application has a specific flow:

- ❖ The user will trigger a request using the internet that goes to the webserver. This can be done through the web browser or user interface on the application.
- ❖ The web server will then forward that request to the specific web application server.

- ❖ The requested task will be performed by the web application server; this includes querying the database or data processing that will generate the required results.
- ❖ The results will be sent to the web server by the web application server; this is in regards to the data processed or the required information.
- ❖ The client will get a response from the webserver; they will get the information that they have requested and it will appear on the user's display.

There are several examples of web applications such as shopping carts, word processors, online forms, file conversions, and scanning, online forms, and email programs like Yahoo and Gmail.

How to Work with Django

Django is used to create web applications. It is specifically meant to create a web application that connects to a database. You can also deal with user management, good security, and internationalization. Some of the common web applications include Disqus, Pinterest, and Instagram. You can use Django as standalone libraries even though it will require extra work. That is the reason why it is not advisable to use it as a standalone.

Django is a combination of different components that work by responding to user requests.

- ❖ The first step is the request-or-response system. The main work is to receive and return web responses. Django will accept all the requests of the URLs and return all the HTML information to the web browser. The page can be in plain text or something better.
- ❖ The web requests will enter the Django application through the URLs. The only entry point for any Django application is the URLs; developers have the control of the available URLs. When you access the URL, Django will enable the viewing.

- All your requests will be processed by the views. Django views are considered to be codes generated from Python when the URL is accessed. Views are something simple like returning a text to the user. The text can be made complex. It can be form processing, credit card processing, and database querying. When the view has completed processing, a web response is sent to the user.
- When web response is returned, the user can access the URL on the browser they will access the response. This could be an HTML web page that shows a combination of images and text, and they are created using the templating system from Django.
- With Django information, there is flexibility to have more applications. You can use that you create a simple blog, mobile applications, or a desktop. Django framework is powered by sites like Instagram and Pinterest.

User Accounts

A user account is on the network server that is used to store the username of the computer, password, and any relevant information. When you have the user account, it will allow you or not to connect with other computers or networks. With a network with multiple users, you will need user accounts. A good example of a user account is your email account.

There are different types of user accounts, regardless of the operating system that you are using. You will be able to trace, authenticate, and monitor all the services. When you install an operating system, it creates user accounts to have access after the installation. After the installation, you will have four user accounts; system account, super user account, regular and guest user account.

- ❖ **System account**: These are accounts that are used to access resources in the system. The operating system will use these accounts to know if a service is allowed to access the resources or not. When they are installed, they create relevant accounts; and after installation, the account will be able to access the needed information. If you are a network or system administrator, you will not need to have any information about the accounts.

- **Super user account**: This account is privileged in the operating system. When one is using Windows, the account is referred to as the Administrator account. When using Linux, the account is the root account, and the operating system will help the user complete different tasks. Tasks are like starting services, creating and deleting new user accounts, installing new software, and changing system files.
- **Regular user account**: This account does not have many privileges and cannot make changes in the system properties and files. They only operate on tasks that they are

authorized like running applications, creating files, and customizing variables.

- ❖ **The Guest user account**: This is the account that has less privilege; you will not be able to change anything with the system. The account is known to perform temporary tasks like playing games, watching movies, or browsing the internet. Using Windows, this account will be created after installation; and in Linux, you will need to create the account manually after installation.

The next step is to know how to create a user account. When you have multiple users using the same computer, you will need to have new user accounts for each user. When using Windows, you can create several accounts. Each of the user accounts has its own settings. It will allow you to control the files separately, and when each user logs in, it will be like their own computer.

The first step in creating a user account is to click on START on the CONTROL PANEL then click on ADD or REMOVE user accounts. Click on CREATE A NEW ACCOUNT and choose the account type. You will enter the account name and then select the account type that you wish to create. The administrator has the privilege to create and change accounts and installing programs. The difference is a standard user cannot perform such tasks. The last step will be to click on the CREATE ACCOUNT button and close the CONTROL PANEL.

How to Style and Deploy an App

There are different deployment options that need to be considered. When an app is developed in the application builder, it is created in the workplace. All the workplaces have IDs and names; all you need is to create an application in the development and then deploy it in production.

During deployment, you will decide where you want the existing ID to be in the workplace, existing HTTP server, or in creating new ones. The deployment options include:

- ❖ You will first create an application that is expressed by end-users. The best way to deploy an application is by creating an Application Express for end users. Then sent the URL and login details to the users. It will work when the user population is tolerant and small.
- ❖ You will need to use the same schema and workplace. You need to export and then import the application, then install that under a different application ID. This strategy will work when there are fewer changes to any known objects.
- ❖ Use the same schema and a different workplace, export all, and then import the applications into another workplace. It will prevent any production and modification by developers.

- Use a different schema and workspace. Export and then import the application into a separate workplace, and install it in a separate schema.
- Use a different database for all variations. Export then import to another oracle application and then install it to a different database and schema.

To deploy an app, in the configuration manager console, click on SOFTWARE LIBRARY. Go to APPLICATION MANAGEMENT and then choose APPLICATION or APPLICATION GROUP.

Choose from an application or application group from the deploy list and click DEPLOY.

Conclusion

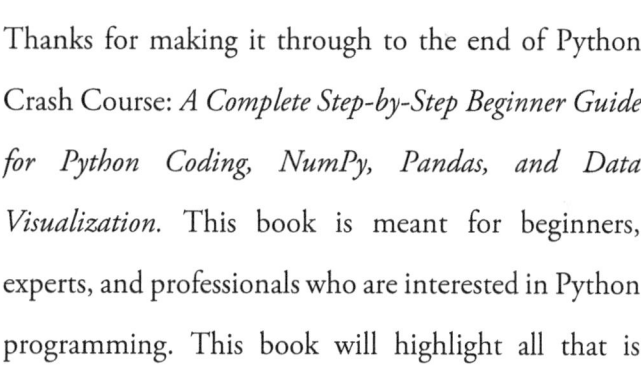

Thanks for making it through to the end of Python Crash Course: *A Complete Step-by-Step Beginner Guide for Python Coding, NumPy, Pandas, and Data Visualization.* This book is meant for beginners, experts, and professionals who are interested in Python programming. This book will highlight all that is needed in Python programming, what Python programming is and its uses.

At this point, you clearly understand who can use Python and its importance to any economists and finance experts. The information will help to know how you can earn as a Python programmer, the basic concepts, and all the terms used in Python programming. You can now start your Python programming for data analysis, how to install Python, and the different places you can learn all this.

With an interactive and educative book, it is easy to understand the operating systems that are used in Python programming. About Linux, OS X, and Windows, you are able to do all the troubleshooting. You know the cost required for Python programming, the courses to learn, and the job you will get after learning. Do you know what a list is? If not, do not worry.

The book will explain all that, how to change, remove, and add the elements. There are data types and visualization. It's about how to generate, download data, and how to work with APIs. The web application is another chapter that is explained, how to work with Django, different user accounts, and how to deploy an app.

We thank you again for choosing to download this book. We believe you did find the book educative and engaging. A positive review on Amazon will be appreciated.

Python for Data Analysis

A Complete Step By Step From Intermediate to Advanced Guide for Python Coding, NumPy, Pandas for Data Analysis. Improve Your Skills Quickly

Introduction

Congratulations on purchasing *Python for Data Analysis* and thank you for doing so.

The following chapters will discuss all of the different parts that we need to know when it comes to performing our own data analysis, and ensuring that we are able to really get some good results in the process. There are a lot of different businesses and industries that are able to work with the data analysis and see the amazing results, and it could be just the thing that you need to take your business to the next level. The information and the insights that you are able to find with data analysis will help you to reach your customers better, find the right customers, know what business decisions to make, and so much more.

We will discuss all of these and more inside of this guidebook.

To start this guidebook, we are going to take a more in-depth look at what data analysis is all about. We will talk about this process and what all it entails, along with some of the benefits of working with this process, and why so many businesses are using it for their own needs as well.

When that part is done, it is time to introduce the Python language. It is possible to work with some of the other coding languages out there to help us handle our data analysis, but none of those are going to provide us with the power and the ease of use, and all of the great extensions and libraries specifically for data analysis like Python can. In this guidebook, we will look at how Python can help us complete our data analysis before diving into some of the different things that you need to do, including some of the coding to help you to get started with programming in this language.

Then it is time for us to dive into some of the libraries and extensions that match up to the Python language and were designed specifically to help us with data analysis. There are a lot of great options here, but we are going to talk about the two most important; the NumPy library and the Pandas library. NumPy is important because it contains the arrays that most of the others will rely on, and Pandas is a good library that can help us with all of the different aspects that we need to focus on when it comes to our data analysis. Learning how to work with both of these is going to be imperative to ensure that we will see a successful data analysis.

To finish everything off, we are going to spend our time looking at some of the steps that come with this data analysis. We will be looking at collecting the data and cleaning it. We will be looking at how to pick out our algorithms and get them all set up and trained before testing them. We will even look at some of the steps to help with our visuals so we can see exactly what happened with the analysis and can use that to our benefit later on. There is information about the importance of machine learning in our data analysis so that we are better able to prepare and do well with our work as well.

As we can see, there are a lot of different parts that have to come together to help us complete data analysis and see the results that we want in the process. And this guidebook is going to take the time to look at how we are able to get this done in a quick and efficient manner. When you are ready to learn more about data analysis and how it works, and about the Python coding language, make sure to check out this guidebook to help you get started.

There are plenty of books on this subject on the market, thanks again for choosing this one! Every effort was made to ensure it is full of as much useful information as possible, please enjoy it!

Chapter 1:
What is a Data Analysis

Before we are able to dive right in and look at what we are able to do with data analysis, it is time for us to take a closer look at what the data analysis is all about. This is a unique process that a lot of companies are going to work with. It allows them to take the enormous amounts of data they are able to collect on a regular basis today and actually learn some of the insights and predictions that are inside of it.

Doing this on our own is going to be impossible. There is just too much data, and it is changing all of the time. Having an individual, or a team, work through this data is going to be a waste of time and won't provide us with the right results anyway. The data will be old by the time we get to it. Data analysis is a process that is going to be able to help with this.

The data analysis will be able to go through all of the steps that we need in order to understand our data, learn what insights are found in that data, and use it to make some good predictions and more in the process. With this in mind, let's take a closer look at what data analysis is all about and how we are able to utilize this for our needs.

What is Data Analytics?

The first step in this process is taking a look at data analytics and what it is all about. To keep it simple, data analytics is going to be the simple science of taking our raw data and analyzing it in order to make some good conclusions about all of that information. Many of the processes and the different techniques of this kind of analytics have been automated into mechanical processes and algorithms that will be able to do some work over this raw data for human consumption.

The techniques that we are going to use when it comes to data analytics can reveal trends and other metrics that would often get lost in the noise and all of the information that we receive. This information can then be used in a manner to help optimize processes to help increase the overall efficiency of a business or system.

There are a lot of benefits that we are able to see when it comes to working with data analysis. When we decide to bring this out, we will be able to notice how helpful it is, and all of the great parts that come with it as well. it is a simple idea, one that can make a big difference in your business but simple enough to understand, but we have to be prepared to go through and really work with the steps to make it work.

It isn't just about picking out a few algorithms and hoping that it is all going to work. There are a number of steps that we need to go through in order to make the analysis behave, and to ensure that it is going to do what we want, whether we are talking about the work that has to be done before the analysis, the actual analysis, and the work afterward.

For example, when we talk about before the analysis, we have to make sure that we collect the right information and information that is higher in quality, that we clean off the data, and that we get it organized so that it works well with the algorithms we choose. During the analysis, we need to focus on the right algorithm to get the work done, and then do several rounds of training and testing to ensure it works. And after the analysis, finding a good way to show off the results and all that is happening is going to be important as well.

Understanding How Data Analytics Works

Data analytics is actually going to be a term that is really broad, and that will encompass many different and diverse types of data analysis. Any type of information that can be used with these techniques will help us to learn some new insights that will be invaluable. Businesses can use these insights to learn more about their customers, to pick out the best products to release, and even to make smarter business decisions in the future.

For example, it is common for some manufacturing companies to work with data analysis. Many of these companies are going to get into the habit of recording the runtime, downtime, and work queue for lots of different machines. They can then analyze all of the data in order to better plan out the workloads they should do, ensuring that the machine and the whole production line is going to work as closely as possible to its peak capacity.

Data analytics is not just used in order to help point out to those in charge of the bottlenecks in production. For example, we are going to find that gaming companies are going to use this data analytics in order to set some good kinds of reward schedules. This is done in a manner to help keep most of the players of a game active.

Content companies will also work with these data analysis in order to work with some of their customers and help to get the readers or consumers to keep on clicking, watching, moving content around, and more. This gives them another click or another view, and then they will be able to earn more money in the same process.

There are actually a number of steps that we are going to work wit in order to work with data analysis. This is going to include some of the following options:

1. The first step that we want to work with here is to determine the data requirements or how

the data is going to be grouped. Data may be separated by demographics, income, age, or gender. The values of this data may be numerical or be divided by category.

2. The second step that we are going to see when it comes to data analytics is the process of collecting all of the data that we want to work with. This can be done through a lot of sources, and we will be able to utilize as many of these as possible in order to gather the information and get it to work well for our needs. You can use online sources, computers, social media, surveys, and more.

3. Once we have had a chance to collect all of the data we want to work with, we then need to actually organize it all. If the data is not organized, which it won't be, if we gather it from a lot of different sources, then we are not going to be able to push it through our chosen algorithms and get accurate results.

   a. There are many methods that we are able to use in order to organize all of that data.

>We can work with a spreadsheet or other form of software that is able to take on some of the statistical data we want.

4. From this step, we are going to clean up all of the data before we work on the analysis. This means that it is going to be checked and scrubbed to make sure there will be no error or duplication and that it is not actually incomplete. This step is a good one to follow in order to get rid of the errors before it is going to be sent over to the analyst to be looked over and worked on by a chosen algorithm.

These are just a few of the options that we are going to pay attention to when it comes to doing data analysis. There are a lot of different parts that we need to bring this together and ensure that we are able to see how it can work and how those companies who decide to work with it can really use it to get ahead and see a foot above the competition in the process.

Data analytics is going to be an important thing to work with because it allows a business to come in and optimize its performance overall. Implementing this kind of process into your model for business means that it is easier to reduce the costs that are present. The company at hand is able to use it to identify some more efficient methods of coding business and storing a lot of data all at once.

A company is also able to take the ideas of data analytics and use it as a way to make some better decisions for their business, and to help them to analyze some of the customer trends and the satisfaction, which is going to lead to new, and better, products and services.

The Different Types of Data Analytics

We are able to take the idea of data analytics and divide it into four different types to make it easier to see what is going on here. The four types of data analytics that we are able to work with includes

1. Descriptive analytics: This is going to describe what has been able to happen over a given period of time. You may take a look to see whether your sales have gone up over the last month or if your views are going up on a video.
2. Diagnostic analytics: This one is a bit different because it is going to focus some more on the reason why something has happened. This is going to involve some data inputs that are more diverse, and you will need to hypothesize a bit. For example, you may ask whether the latest campaign had any impact on your sales.
3. Predictive analytics: This is going to take a look at what we think is going to happen in the near term. It may look at how sales did the last time the summer was hot, and then it will look at how likely it is going to be really hot during summer again.

4. Prescriptive analytics: This is going to suggest a course of action. If it is likely that we are going to get a warm summer again and we measure it based on an average of five weather models, then you would rearrange your business so that you can keep up with the demand.

Data analytics is going to take some time to underpin some of the other quality control systems that are found in the world of finances. One of these quality control programs that will often work well with data analysis is going to Six Sigma. This is a whole program that helps us to find some of the waste that is found in the business, and then learn how to reduce this to help save money and become more efficient.

The idea with both of these is that if you are not able to go through and measure something properly, whether you are looking at your own weight or the number of defects that are going to show up per million on the production line, then it is going to be impossible for the company to really optimize it.

There are also a lot of different companies that have decided to adopt data analytics in their own business model in order to get some of the best results. One of the first sectors that we can look at that has used data analytics is hospitality and travel. These are going to need a lot of quick turnarounds to see some good results, and this industry is able to go through and collect some data about the customers to figure out where the problems, if there are any problems, lie, and how we are able to fix them early on.

Another place where we are going to be able to see the benefits of data analytics in the world of healthcare. This is going to be able to combine together the use of high volumes of structured and unstructured data, and then will work the data analytics and all of the techniques that come with it to help make some smart decisions.

In a similar manner, the retail industry, which may be an industry that we don't think that much about when it comes to working in data analytics, is going to work here as well. They will gather up lots of data in order to keep up with the demands of their customers, which are always changing. The information that these retailers are able to collect and analyze can make it easier to identify some trends, recommend the right products, and overall help to increase the profits of that company.

These are just a few of the companies that are going to benefit from working with data analytics to help them out. There are a lot of different methods and techniques that we are able to use to make this work. But when we are able to put the parts together, and we make sure that we have the right types of data, we will be able to handle all of this and get some of the best insights to steer our predictions in no time.

Chapter 2: Reasons to Work with a Data Analysis

Now that we know a little bit more about working with data analysis and why this is such a good thing to work with overall, it is time for us to take a look at why a company would want to work with a data analysis overall. It is not the process that many companies are used to working with. When we learn how to make it work, though, and see some of the benefits that we are able to get out of it, we will find that it is an amazing option to handle as well.

Data is going to be available through a lot of different options. We can look at data through mobile app usage, digital clicks, interactions that happen on social media, and so more. This is all going to contribute to a unique data fingerprint that is going to be just their owner. Companies have to be able to learn the best way to take advantage of all of this to provide the customers with the kind of experience that the customer is looking for.

At the same time, companies are also finding that it is good for them to be more aware that creating the most engaging experience for the customer is going to provide them with some of the competitive advantages that they need. When we work with some advanced analytics, companies re able to make better use of their user and customer experience data. And this is going to lead to a lot of higher satisfaction and loyalty with the customers over time.

The good news is that there are a few benefits that any company will be able to experience when they use this data analysis. It is such a beneficial process, even though it can take some time, that it is definitely worth your time to learn more about how this works and what you are able to do with it. Some of the benefits that we are going to be able to notice when it comes to working with a data analysis includes

1. It can deliver the right products.

One of the ways that you are able to make some money for your business is to sell products and services. And with all of the competition that is out there, you need to make sure that you are releasing the right kinds of products in order to get started. There are other competitors out there, and customers sometimes don't realize what products they would most like. For example, if you bring out a new product like Amazon has done several times with products in the past like the Kindle, you need to be innovative and figure out what the customer would like before they even know.

Effective data collection, along with some good analytics, is going to make sure that a company is able to stay as competitive as possible. This can be especially important at any time that there is a newly developed technology or the customers come in with changes to their demands. This is also a good way to anticipate the demands of the market in order to provide the right products before they are even requested in the long run.

2. Personalization and service

With all of the competition out there, it is important that we are able to go through and provide something that is unique to our customers. It is too easy to get complacent, but we have to remember that there are a lot of different businesses out there who are able and willing to reach the niche of customers if you won't. And one of the best ways that you are able to really provide the best to the customers and get them to notice you some more, at least more than the competition, is to add in some personalize and service that others are not providing.

Companies have to be good and responsive in order to cope with a lot of the volatility that is created by their customers, especially the ones that are going to engage through some of the different digital technologies today. Being able to react in a manner that is more real-time, and can make the customer feel that your company really values them in a personal manner is going to be possible, but we have to make sure that we do this through advanced analytics.

Big data is going to help us gain the opportunity to interact with others based on the personality of that individual customer. It is going to help us do this by understanding more about the attitudes of the customer and then will consider some of the other factors, including real-time location, to help us deliver some personalization in a service environment that may rely on a bunch of different channels as well.

3. Helps us to be proactive and anticipate the needs of customers

Another reason that we would want to work with data analysis is that it is going to help us be more proactive when it comes to anticipating the needs of our customers. By sharing their own data with businesses, customers are going to expect that these companies know them a lot better. They expect to see relevant interaction and get a seamless experience across all of the touchpoints. This is something that your company is going to need to work in order to attract more customers in the future.

When you are able to go through and understand the needs of the customers, you will find that it is a lot easier to keep and maintain your customers as well. Companies are able to use this in order to understand the needs of their customers and then can optimize the customer experience, resulting in relationships that are strong and longstanding.

4. Optimize and then improve operational efficiency

When it comes to how well your business is able to perform, and the amount of money and time you are wasting, we want to make sure that we can keep this number down as much as possible. This is the best way to ensure that we can provide a good product to the customer and that we will be able to get them interested in sticking around. If we are not optimized as much as possible, then unnecessary costs are going to add up, and we may never get a chance to grow and do well because our product will be too expensive to work with.

Applying analytics for designing and controlling the process, and then doing what you can to optimize the operations of your business is going to ensure the efficiency and effectiveness so that we can fulfill the expectations of the customer, while still achieving some operational excellence in the process.

There are a number of ways that we are able to get this done. For example, it is possible for a business to work with a number of advanced analytics techniques so that they can improve their own productivity, efficiency, and field operations. And this is also a method that we can work with to figure out the best way to optimize the workforce of the customer based on the demands of the customers and their business needs.

If you are able to do a little bit of work and really optimize your business, and ensure that you are operating in a manner that reaches all of the demand of the customer without wasting money and having too much going on that doesn't need to be there, then your business is going to be more efficient. You will only spend money when it is needed, and this can help you to really get some great results in the process.

5. Mitigating risk and fraud

As a business, these are going to be two big things that we need to focus our time on. The more risk that your company takes on, the harder it is going to be to keep making money. A bit of risk is going to be fine and a normal part of running a business (though data analysis can help you to reduce the amount of risk that you are dealing with), but you never want to take on too much risk, or you will run your business into the ground.

Another thing to worry about, especially if you are in the financial industry, is the idea of fraud. When people try to commit fraud, it is going to harm the business and their other customers as well. Fraud has been responsible for millions of lost dollars over the years, so it makes sense that we would want to work with data analytics in order to reduce the amount of fraud that is going on and what we would like to do with it.

Security and fraud analytics, which can be done with data analysis, are going to aim to help us protect all of the intellectual, financial, and physical assets from being misused by any kind of internal and external threats. Efficient data and efficient analytics working together will be able to deliver what we need when it comes to optimum levels of fraud prevention and overall organizational security.

Data management is going to be a big part of all of this, and when we are able to use that management along with some efficient and transparent reporting of incidents of fraud along the way, this is going to help us get the improved fraud risk management processes that we want. In addition, when we are able to integrate and correlate all of our data throughout the whole business, no matter how big or small it is, we are able to offer a new and unified view of how fraud happens in the business based on the different lines of the business, the transactions, and the products at hand.

These are just a few of the different options that we are able to work with when it is time to handle data analysis. And no matter what kind of business you are in the first place, all five of the benefits above are going to be important to helping you to get things done while ensuring that you are offering a high-quality product to your customers in a timely and cost-effective manner.

There are other methods that you are able to utilize to help you to make plans for your business and to make it easier to come up with big decisions while reaching your customers and releasing products that they want. But none are going to be as effective as what we are going to see when we work with data analysis. That is why we are going to spend some time in this guidebook learning more about the different parts of Data analysis, how we can work with the Python language to make it more efficient, and so much more.

Chapter 3: How Does Python Fit Into This?

The next thing on our list that we need to focus on is how we can work with Python in order to complete the data analysis that we would like. There are a lot of different parts that come with our data analysis, and having it all come together, is going to take us some time and some good planning in the process. At one point, though, we will need to go through and make sure that we are working with a programming language, one that is versatile and strong, and one that is going to help us to run our algorithms as we go.

Our algorithms are very important to how well the data analysis will work. These are the pars that will take ahold of our data, and look through it all, sorting it through and telling us the insights or the patterns that are inside of it. But to get these to work well and to make sure that we are not going to end up with a big mess in the end and inaccurate results, we need to make sure that we are choosing a good and a strong language to get it done.

There are a lot of different coding languages that we are able to work with, and each one is going to bring about its own positives and negatives that we need to deal with. If you hear about the idea of coding and learning how to do a programming language, and it makes you nervous and anxious, have no fear. There are a lot of different languages that we are able to focus on in order to help us to handle our algorithms and get the best results when we want to work with our data analysis.

The number one language that is going to work for data analysis, and the machine learning that we need to accomplish in order to handle these algorithms, is

Python. As we are going to explore in this chapter, there are a lot of benefits that come with using Python, whether you just want to learn the basics of coding, or you are interested in handling something as complicated at data analysis. Let's dive in and see what some of these benefits are all about.

Python is an easy language to work with. If you are someone who has never done anything with coding before, and you are a bit nervous about getting started, and what that will be like, then the Python language is going to be one of the best options to help you get it off to a good start.

There are many options in coding languages out there, but a lot of them are going to be kind of difficult to learn. They are often reserved for some of the more complicated types of coding that you want to use, and you can build them later. But if you are a complete beginner in coding, then Python is going to be the best option for you. It is simple to read and use, and we will look at a few codes in the next chapter to help show how this is going to work for us. This can take some of the stress out of the whole process as well when it is time to learn a brand new coding language to work with data analysis.

Python has a large library that makes learning the codes easier. You will be amazed at how much power is going to be found when you work with Python, and how many options and functions are found in this language as well. whether you are a beginner or looking to add a few other parts and coding languages to your skill set, you will find that the traditional Python library is going to have all of the parts that you need to be more successful with it.

There are a lot of extensions and other libraries that work with Python that are specifically designed to enhance its capabilities and make it work better for a good data analysis. Even though the traditional library that comes with Python is going to include a lot of the power and more that you want with coding, there are other extensions that make sure you are able to complete some of the processes that you want with data science, data analysis, and even machine learning. Python, more than any other language, has a lot of these options, which can make it so much easier overall to get your work done.

There is a lot of power that you are able to enjoy when it is time to work on Python. Even though we have spent some time talking about how easy the Python language is going to be to learn, we have to remember that ease of use does not mean that you are missing out on power. The good news is that Python is going to come with a lot of power, and you will be able to use it in order to handle almost any project that you would like along the way.

The community of Python is going to be large, allowing even a beginner to get some of the assistance that they need along the way. This may not seem like a big deal, but when you are working on learning how to work with a new language, it is going to prove to be invaluable. Any time that you need to learn something new that you have a new question, or you get stuck, and you are not able to figure out how to get things fixed and working again, that community is going to be the answer that you need.

The community is going to include programmers from all around the world. And often, they will have a lot of different experience levels when it comes to how much they know how to do with coding. As a beginner, you can easily join and be included. And there are many programmers who are more advanced who are willing to share some of their time and knowledge with you as well. This helps to facilitate some of the work that you want to accomplish and can make it easier to learn something new.

You can use Python with some of the other languages that are sometimes a necessity when working with data analysis. For the most part, Python is going to work just fine with some of the work that you want to do with sorting, organizing, fixing, testing, training, and creating with data analysis. But there are a few algorithms that are going to perform a bit better when we work with some other coding languages.

The neat thing is that you can often use some of the libraries and extensions that come with Python to help fix this issue. You can write out the codes in the Python language, keeping it as easy and simple as possible, and then the extension is going to come in and take over, converting the language over to something else, and then executing it all for you. It is as simple as that for you to continue using the Python language in the way that you would like and still get the work done that is necessary.

Python works really well when it comes to handling some machine learning, which is often the core component that we see with the algorithms that run data analysis. While the focus of this guidebook is more about the basics of Python and of data analysis, we will find that when it comes to working on the algorithms that we want to handle in all of this, they are going to be run through the use of machine learning.

Machine learning is simply a process that helps take a program or even a whole system and set it up so that it is able to run on its own. The programmer will not have to come in and figure out all of the ways the system should behave. The system will be able to take the information that it gathers, and what it learns from the user, and use that to become smarter and better at its job overall. It is the main technology that is going to help us to run our algorithms so we can learn the patterns and insights that are needed in data analysis.

And the main language that is used to help create some of these machine learning algorithms in Python. Python can be used for other parts of the data analysis process, but you will also find that it is useful for helping us to create, train, and test the algorithms, ensuring that they are going to behave in the proper manner as well.

As we can see, there are a lot of different benefits that you will be able to enjoy when it comes to using Python. You can enjoy Python whether you are looking to increase some of your own knowledge base of programming and more, or if you are just looking for something to add to your skill sets. But it also works well for things like machine learning and data analysis, which are all going to be combined together for many of the projects that we want.

There may be a few other languages out there that we are able to work with that can handle our algorithms and may have some extensions and libraries that work with them to get the work done. But none are going to be as easy to use, as efficient to work with or provide the benefits that we are looking for, as we are able to find with the Python language. If you are looking for something that is simple to work with and will provide you with all of the benefits of learning how to program without taking years or months to figure out, then Python is the right one to use.

Don't worry if you have never done anything with coding in the past, though. Not only are we spending this chapter talking about how Python is beneficial as a coding language to learn, and how it is able to help us with some of the work that we want to do with data analysis, you will also find that it is going to be easy to learn. And the next chapter is going to take a look at some of the basics that you need to know in order to get started with coding in Python and making this work for your coding needs.

Chapter 4:
Some of the Basic Codes in Python

Now that we have had a chance to look at Python and some of the benefits that come with it to ensure we get the full reasons why someone would want to use it for data analysis, it is time for us to go through some of the basics of writing code in Python. There are a lot of different parts that are all going to come together to help us make sure that we are writing our codes out well, and that we actually learn what Python is all about. That is why we are going to take some time to explore these in this chapter so we can use them later on in our data analysis.

Some of the different parts that you need to know when it comes to writing out codes in Python include:

The Keywords

The first part that we need to take a look at in here is the keywords. These are going to be special words, ones that are reserved, to help make sure that the compiler knows what commands it is supposed to follow along the way. There are a number of keywords that we are able to work within Python, and if we do not use them in the proper manner. If we go through and use the keywords at the wrong place, then you will end up with errors in your code, and it will not behave properly. But when this is done in the right location, then the compiler will know exactly what you are trying to get it to do.

Python Comments

The next thing that we need to take a look at in the comments. These are going to be unique parts of any code that allow you to add in a little bit of a note or information into the code without it actually affecting the code or causing it to have an error.

If you would like to name a certain part of the code, or you want to leave a little message for yourself, or for another programmer who would take a look through your information and your code. You can explain what is going through that part of the code for yourself or someone else, get it a different name, or something else.

Working on the comments is going to be simple to work with. Each code is going to work with these comments in a slightly different manner, but in the Python language, we just need to use the # symbol ahead of the comment. You can have the comment be as long or short as you would like, and you can have as many of these in your code as you would like as well. The rule is to just keep this to a minimum as much as possible, though, to ensure the code stays nice and clean along the way.

Python as an OOP Language

One thing that is unique about the Python language, along with a few others that are similar to it, is that this language is considered an object-oriented programming language, or OOP. This is going to be useful for you as a beginner because it ensures that your codes stay nice and organized along the way, and will make it easier for us to ensure the codes are going to behave in the way that we want them to.

Basically, this means that Python is going to be divided up into classes and objects to add to some organizations. The classes will be like containers in the code, there to help hold onto other parts that are similar to one another, or belong with one another in the code. You can add in as many of these classes as you would like along the way to help organize your objects, and we will take a look at some of the different ways that you can create these classes as well.

Python programming

Then we can move on to the objects. The objects are going to be anything that we can place into the classes that we created. They will correspond to real objects that we find out in the world, so we won't have to deal with a bunch of abstract ideas along the way either. We will create the class that we want and then add in the objects to keep them together until they are called.

We are able to put in any kind of objects that we want into a class, as long as it makes sense for that object to be there. If someone else takes a look at the class that we work with, and they look at the objects, they should be able to tell why those specific objects are in the class together.

This doesn't mean that the objects in a class have to be identical to one another. But it should make sense why one object goes into that class, and another would not be put in. For example, you can have a class that includes farm animals and then add in as many of these animals as you want. You are not restricted to just putting spotted cows in a class.

How to Write a Class

The next thing that we need to take a look at here is how to write out some of our own classes in Python. Python is considered an object-oriented programming language, as we talked about above. Almost everything that we work within Python is going to be an object with the right methods and properties in place. A class is going to be like a blueprint or an object constructor that we are able to use when it is time to create the objects that we want to work with.

The good news is that creating a new class is not something that has to be all that difficult. We can create a simple class, and all that we need for this is the keyword of class. The code that we can use for this one includes:

```
class MyClass:
  x = 5
```

Once the class is done and created, we then need to go through and actually create an object that we are able to add to what we would like to have into that class. We are going to use the class that we created above, which is now known as myClass, to help us create objects. And we are able to do this with the following code:

```
p1 = MyClass()
print(p1.x)
```

While we are here, we are going to take a look at another function that we are able to introduce to our class that can make it work out better than it would on its own. The examples that we used above are going to be the classes and objects as we can use them in Python, but they are still in a pretty simple form and are not going to be that useful in most of the forms that we want to write out.

To help us get a better understanding of the meaning of these classes and what we are able to do with them, we need to understand one of the functions that have been built-in with Python, and that is the function of __init__().

All classes are going to have this function. This is because it is going to be important to help us get things done. This particular function is going to be executed as soon as we start to initiate the class as well.

We want to be able to work with this function in order to help assign some values to the properties of our objects, or to other operations that are necessary to do when we try to create the object. In the code that we are going to have below, we are going to create a class that we will name as Person, and then we will use the function above that we have been talking about to help us assign the values necessary for name and age:

```
class Person:
  def __init__(self, name, age):
    self.name = name
    self.age = age

p1 = Person("John", 36)

print(p1.name)
print(p1.age)
```

The next thing on the list that we need to explore is the object methods. These will be a bit different than the objects that we talked about above, but they are still important for us to spend some time on when we want to create our codes.

Objects can work on their own, or we can use them and make sure they contain methods. Methods are going to be found in objects, and this is when they are going to specifically be a function that will belong back to the object.

Now we are going to work on creating one of these object methods in that Person class we had before. We will also go through and insert a function that will print out a greeting for us and then execute it on the p1 object below:

```
class Person:
  def __init__(self, name, age):
    self.name = name
    self.age = age

  def myfunc(self):
    print("Hello my name is " + self.name)

p1 = Person("John", 36)
p1.myfunc()
```

and finally, we need to look at what is known as the self parameter. There are a lot of times when the parameter is going to be important to the code that we want to write out on a regular basis, and working with this specific parameter is going to be useful in a lot of the codes that we want to create.

To start, the "self" parameter is going to be a good reference that we can use to the current instance of our class. It is also going to be used to help access some of the variables that will belong to the class.

Of course, keep in mind here that we do not need to name this parameter as "self" to make it work. You are able to go through and give it any kind of name that you would like along the way. Just remember for it to work, it has to come in as the first parameter of any function that is found in your class. A good example of how to work with this particular type of parameter includes

```
class Person:
  def __init__(mysillyobject, name, age):
    mysillyobject.name = name
    mysillyobject.age = age
```

```
def myfunc(abc):
  print("Hello my name is " + abc.name)

p1 = Person("John", 36)
p1.myfunc()
```

Python Functions

Now that we have a better idea of how the classes are going to work in Python and why these are so important to some of the work that we want to create in this language, it is time to move on to some of the other parts of coding that are important for our goals as well. in particular, we are going to spend a bit of time looking at the steps that we are able to follow in order to create a function in the Python language.

A function, to start with, is just going to be a block of code, any block of code, which is only going to run when the compiler calls it out. You are able to pass on data, which will be known as a parameter, over to your function to ensure that it is going to work in the manner that you want. And then, as the function continues to do its job, it is able to return data as a result as well.

With this in mind, we need to take a look at some of the steps that we are able to use in order to create and then call one of the functions that we want to work with. This is fairly simple because we are able to define one of these functions with the use of the def keyword. The code that you can use to create one of these functions includes:

```
def my_function():
  print("Hello from a function")
```

Once the function is created and ready to go, it is then time for us to go through and call up a function. To call this function, we need to make sure that we rely on the name of the function (whichever name we decided to give to the function), and put it all into parenthesis. The code that we are able to use for this one will be below:

```
def my_function():
  print("Hello from a function")
```

my_function()

While we are here, we need to take a closer look at something that is known as the arguments that come with functions. Some of the information that we pass over to the functions can be done more like an argument instead. Arguments are going to be specified after the name of the function, inside of our parenthesis to make sure that things are organized and ready to go. You are able to add in as many of these arguments as you would like, we just need to make sure that they have been separated out with a comma.

Now it is time for us to go through and see a good example of how this is going to work. The code that we will focus on here is going to have a function that just has one argument, which is known as (fname) when we are able to call up the function, we will pass along the first name, which is the going to be used inside of the function to help us get the full name printed off as well. The way that we would write out this code is below:

```
def my_function(fname):
 print(fname + " Refsnes")

my_function("Emil")
my_function("Tobias")
my_function("Linus")
```

now that we have brought up both the idea of a parameter and that of an argument, we need to figure out which one is going to be the best one to use for our codes. The terms of argument and parameter can be used for the same thing because both of them are going to include information that is passed on over to the function.

When we look at this from the perspective of the function, the parameter is going to be a variable that is listed inside of the parentheses in the definition of the function. The argument, on the other hand, is going to be the value that has been sent to the function when it is called out. We can use both in a similar manner along the way, though.

We can also work with the idea that is known as recursion. Python is also going to accept what is known as function recursion, which means that the defined function is able to come through and call itself.

Recursion is going to be a common concept in programming and mathematics. It means that a function is going to call itself. This has the benefit of allowing programming to loop through the data to reach the result that we are working with.

If you want to work with recursion, you need to be careful with the work that you handle here. It is easy to mess up and start writing a function that is never going to terminate, or one that is going to use too much memory or processing power to get the work done. However, when it is written out in the correct manner, it is possible for recursion to be efficient, and an elegant approach, mathematically, when you do your programming.

We are going to take a look at how to work with recursion below. This will make it easier for a beginner to get started learning how this works without having to worry as much about whether it is all going to work out well or not. The coding that we can use for this kind of recursion includes:

```
def tri_recursion(k):
  if(k>0):
    result = k+tri_recursion(k-1)
    print(result)
  else:
    result = 0
  return result

print("\n\nRecursion Example Results")
tri_recursion(6)
```

Python Variables

Now it is time for us to move on and take a look at how we are able to create some of the variables in our code, and why these are so important to coding in Python as well. Python variables are a simple idea. They are set up in order t hold onto a small spot in the memory of our computer as well. then we can assign a value over to it, just using an equal sign, so that something is actually held in the space of memory.

Variables are going to be containers that we can use to store the values of data. Unlike some of the other programming languages that you may use in the past, Python is not going to come with a command that will declare that variable for you. Instead, the variable is going to just be created the moment that you first give value over to it. A good example of how the code will look when you assign a value over to it is below:

```
x = 5
y = "John"
print(x)
print(y)
```

Variables do not need to have any declaration, and they don't have to be associated back to any particular type. We are even able to go through and change the type after we set them up. They are a lot easier to work with than what we may see in some of the other options of coding out there.

There will be a few rules that we have to keep in place when it is time to name the variable we want to use. You can make it easy and give the variable a short name, or you can go through and give it a name that is more descriptive of what it is holding onto. Some of the rules that we are able to utilize when it comes to our Python variables will include:

1. The name of the variable has to start with a letter or the underscore character.
2. A variable name is not allowed to start with a number.
3. A variable name can only contain things like alpha-numeric characters and the underscore, so nothing special in there.
4. The name recognizes case sensitivity. This means that there will be a difference between BLUE, Blue, and blue in this language.

Lists vs. Dictionaries

Another topic that is going to show up when we work with Python is the differences between a list and a dictionary, and even a tuple. First, we are going to explore what the lists are like. The list is going to actually have the most versatility when it comes to types of objects that are used in Python. Some of the things that we will notice when working on these lists include

1. A list is going to be an ordered and mutable sequence of items. Because of this, it is something that we are able to slice, index, and change along the way. Each element is something that we are able to access using the position it has on the list. Python lists are going to work for most of the collection data structures, and since they are found as built-in, you do not have to go through the process of manually creating them.
2. Lists are going to be used for any object type, from strings to numbers and to more lists as well.
3. They are going to be accessed just like a string, which means that they are simple to use, and they will be variable in length. We are able to

see them shrink and grow automatically as we use them.
4. List variables are going to be declared when we work with the brackets, and then the name of the variable will be ahead of it.

Another option to explore is known as a tuple. Tuples are going to be used in Python to help hold together more than one object. Think of this as something that is similar to the list, but it is not going to have the extensive functionality that the list class is going to provide to us. One of the major features that we will like about these tuples is that they are going to be immutable, similar to strings, which means we are not able to modify them.

Even though modification is not allowed here, you are able to take portions of some of the existing tuples and use it to make a new tuple. Lists are going to be declared with a square bracket, and then we are able to change them as needed. However, the tuple is going to be found in the parentheses, and we are not able to change them at all.

And third on the list in the dictionary. This one is a bit unique in Python as well because it is going to focus on things in a different manner. The dictionary is going to rely mostly on what is known as the key: value pair, which is similar to what we would know as an associative array if you have worked in other programming languages.

A good way to think about the dictionary is like an address book where we are going to be able to find the address or the contact details of a person simply by knowing their name. With the dictionary, we are going to associate the keys or the name, with the values, or the details, to get what we want in the process. We must note here, though, that the key has to be unique for this to work, similar to how we are not able to find the right information on a person if we have two individuals with the same name.

Creating a Simple Loop

There are actually a few different types of loops that we are able to work with when it comes to Python. These are going to be nice because they take out some of the work. If there is a part of the code that you would like to see repeat itself a bunch of times, rather than rewriting out that part of code over and over again, we would simply turn it into a loop. In specific, we are going to take a look at what the for loop is about and how we can utilize this for our needs too.

To start, the for loop is going to be used to help us iterate over one of the sequences that we want to use. This could be a string, a set, a dictionary, a tuple, or a list. This is going to be less like the keyword that we see with other coding languages, and it is more like the iterator method for other OOP languages.

When we focus on the for loop, we are going to spend some time executing a set of specific statements that we want to see taken care of. This is going to happen one time for each item on the list, tuple, or set. A good example that we can look at here is below:

```
fruits = ["apple", "banana", "cherry"]
for x in fruits:
  print(x)
```

Now in some cases, we also have to make sure that we add in a break statement. This will ensure that the code will know where to stop and that it is not going to keep going in an endless loop that we are not able to stop. This will effectively freeze up our computers and make it hard to work with them without exiting the whole program. Set up the broken part in this to ensure that it will behave in the manner that you want.

The If Else Statement in Decision Control

There will be some situations where you will want to let the computer make a decision on its own. This will often be a decision that is based on the input that the user provides to the computer. You can set up some conditions to tell the computer how to behave, or the program how to behave. But since you are not able to guess all of the potential inputs that the user is going to work with, we need to work with what is known as the decision control statements.

There are three main ones in the Python language. There is the if statement, the if else statement, and the elif statement. All of these are going to work in slightly different manners and can be important based on the information that we want to include in our statements. But we are going to spend our time here looking at the method that is used the most in these decision control statements, and that is the if else statement.

This statement is going to have at least two possible outcomes. If the input from the user is true based on the conditions that you set, then the if part of the statement is going to be applied and executed. If the input of the user is not true based on the conditions that you set, then the computer is going to execute the else statement.

We can also go down the line with this one a few times and have a few different if statements. Then the program is going to just check each one and determine if the input is true based on that condition. If it is, then that is the statement that the compiler will execute. If it is not, then it goes all the way down the line until it reaches the else statement, and that will be the one that is executed.

The syntax that we are able to use for this one will be below

```
if expression:
   statement(s)
else:
   statement(s)
```

The cool thing here is that we are able to take this one a bit further if we would like. A good example of how to write out some codes that work with our if else statement would be the two options below:

```python
#!/usr/bin/python

var1 = 100
if var1:
   print "1 - Got a true expression value"
   print var1
else:
   print "1 - Got a false expression value"
   print var1

var2 = 0
if var2:
   print "2 - Got a true expression value"
   print var2
else:
   print "2 - Got a false expression value"
   print var2

print "Goodbye!"
```

Can I Create an Inheritance?

The final thing that we are going to look at in this part about Python and how to handle it is the inheritance in Python. Inheritances in Python will allow us to define a class that is able to inherit all of the properties and the methods from the class that we created in the past already. There are two main parts that come with the inheritance, and these include the parent class and the child class.

The parent class is going to be the original class or the one that is being inherited from. You will sometimes see that it is called the base class. Then there is the child class. This is going to be the class we work with that will inherit from another class. We can sometimes call it the derived class.

With this in mind, we are going to take a look at some of the steps that we can use in order to create our own parent class. Any class can technically be one of these parent classes. Because of this, the syntax that you are going to use is similar to what we talked about earlier when we created just a simple class. The code that you can use includes:

```python
class Person:
  def __init__(self, fname, lname):
    self.firstname = fname
    self.lastname = lname

  def printname(self):
    print(self.firstname, self.lastname)
```

#Use the Person class to create an object and then execute the printname method:

```python
x = Person("John", "Doe")
x.printname()
```

Now that we have gone through and created the parent class and we have that all set up, it is time for us to go through and create the child class that we want to work with. This is going to be the class that takes things from the original parent class and makes it unique and new. We can take things away and add in more without messing with the parent class at all, but we will still use some of the basis of the parent class here.

Now we want to go through the process of creating that child class. To help us create a class that is able to handle and inherit the functionality from another class, we want to make sure that we send the parent class as the parameter we want to use when creating the child class. The code that we are able to use to make this happen includes:

```
class Student(Person):
 pass
```

Remember that __init__() function that we talked about earlier? We need to bring that back in here to help us out. In the codes above, we have simply created a child class that is going to inherit all of the methods and properties from the original code. We want to bring in this function to the child class rather than working with the pass keyword because this function is going to be called any time that we want to use the class to create a new object. This will just make it all easier down the line. The code that we want to use to make this happen includes:

```
class Student(Person):
  def __init__(self, fname, lname):
    #add properties etc.
```

At some point, we are going to want to add some properties to the child class. This allows us to not just work with the exact code that we had before. But we will be able to go through and make some of the changes to this new child code as some of the functionality of the parent code, but there will be some differences as well so that we can have it be brand new and working for or needs. The code that we can use when we would like to add in some properties to our child class includes:

```python
class Student(Person):
  def __init__(self, fname, lname):
    super().__init__(fname, lname)
    self.graduationyear = 2019
```

in addition to working with the properties that we want to add into the code, we need to go through and add in some of the right methods as well. these are slightly different, but we are able to work with it to help our child class act in the manner that we want. The example that we are going to take a look at below will add in a method that we will name as "welcome" to the class that is labeled as "Student". The code that we want to take a look at to make this happen is below:

```python
class Student(Person):
  def __init__(self, fname, lname, year):
    super().__init__(fname, lname)
    self.graduationyear = year

  def welcome(self):
    print("Welcome", self.firstname, self.lastname, "to the class of", self.graduationyear)
```

If you go through and add in a method that goes to your child class with the same name as a function in the parent class, you have to note that the inheritance of that parenting method is going to be overridden, so keep that in mind when you get started.

As we can see, there are a lot of different parts that are going to come into play when we are working with the Python language. And all of these codes can help you to learn more about how this language works, and what we are able to do with it overall. After you get some practice with this, you will be ready to go if you decide to work with data analysis, and you get ready to create your own algorithms to make this happen.

Chapter 5: What is the NumPy Library

Now it is time for us to take a look at one of the great libraries that we can work with when it comes to using Python and getting our data analysis to work well for our needs. NumPy is one of the first that we can look at, and it is going to be one of the best. It is actually going to be the basis that we can see with some of the other important libraries that we will discuss later on, or other data analysis libraries, so it is worth our time to take a look at it.

To start with, NumPy is a library that is used in Python. We are able to use it for a number of different reasons, including numerical as well as scientific computing if we need it. For the most part, though, it is going to be used to help us compute our array s in a quick and efficient manner. We will have it based and written out in the Python and the C language.

Even though this is a language that works for the C language as well, this is going to be a basic data analysis library that we are going to use with Python, and the word NumPy is going to stand for Numerical Python. We are going to bring out this library to help us to process any of the homogeneous multidimensional arrays that we want to handle.

This library is going to be one of the core libraries that is used for different scientific computations. This means that it is going to have a powerful array of objects that are multidimensional, and it will integrate some tools that are useful when it is time to really work with these arrays as well.

You will quickly find that when you work with the data analysis that we have been talking about that NumPy is going to be useful in almost all of the scientific programming that we try to do with Python, including things like statistics, machine learning, and bioinformatics. It is also going to provide us with some good functionality that we are able to work with, functionality that is able to work well will run in an efficient manner, and is well written in the process.

As we mentioned before, this is going to be a library that is focused mainly on performing some of the mathematical operations that we need to use on contiguous arrays, much like the arrays that are found in a few other languages, including what is seen in the C language. This means that we are able to use NumPy to help us manipulate some of our numerical data as well

Understanding More About NumPy

You will quickly find that outside of the standard Python library. The NumPy library is going to be one of the most used libraries in Python. Data science techniques and algorithms of all kinds are going to need work to be done by the matrices, large size arrays, and lots of numerical computation in order to look through their data and learn what is there. And NumPy is going to be able to take on this job in a seamless manner.

This library is really basic, but it is still going to be important when it comes to handling some of the scientific computing that we want to do with Python. Plus, it will not take that long working with data science and data analysis before you find that this is going to be the library that other data analysis libraries are going to be dependent on.

Some of the other major libraries are going to be dependent on the arrays in NumPy as their inputs and outputs. In addition to this, it is also going to provide some functions that are going to allow developers a way for developers to perform all of the basic and the advanced functions that they would like, whether we are talking about statistics or mathematics, especially when we are dealing with multi-dimensional arrays and matrices, without needing to use as many lines of codes to get it all done.

When we compare these arrays with the lists that we talked about earlier with Python, you will find that the arrays are going to be much faster. But Python lists do have an advantage over the arrays because they are more flexible as you are only able to store the same data type in each column when we are working with the arrays.

There are a few features that you are going to enjoy when it is time to work with the NumPy library. Some of the main features that you will enjoy the most will include:

1. The NumPy library is going to be a combination of Python and C language,
2. This is going to consist of arrays that are homogeneous and multi-dimensional.

Ndarray is part of this as well, which will be n-dimensional arrays as well.

3. It is going to work on a lot of different functions for arrays if you would like.
4. It can also help us to reshape the arrays. It also allows Python to have a way to work as an alternative to MATLAB.

There are a lot of reasons why we would want to work with NumPy rather than having to pick one of the other libraries that are out there along the way. We will use the array in NumPy for the work that we are doing with Python instead of a list. And some of the reasons for this include it is convenient to work with, it is going to perform faster than other methods, and it is going to use less memory overall.

All of these are going to be important when we are trying to do some of the algorithms that we need in data analysis. And mostly, you will notice that the arrays are going to be the number one thing that we utilize when it is time to work with this library as well.

There are a few other things that we need to explore when it comes to how we are able to work with the NumPy library. First, the NumPy array is going to take up a lot less space than other options. The arrays that we have been talking about in this chapter are going to be a lot smaller when it comes to size than we will see with the lists in Python. A list with this language is able to take about 20MB of space, which is going to really take up space on your computer if you work with a few of these.

On the other hand, we are able to create an array, and it is only going to take about 4 MB. If you need to use a lot of different arrays as you go through, and they are going to fit better on the space of your memory overall. Arrays are also going to be easier to access when you would like to read and write on them later on.

In addition, the performance when it comes to speed, you will find that the NumPy arrays are going to be great. It is going to be able to perform a lot faster when it comes to computations than what we find with the Python lists. Because this library is considered open-sourced, it is not going to cost you anything to get started with. Then it also has the benefit of working with the popular Python programming language, which has high-quality libraries for almost all of the tasks that you want to accomplish.

All of these are great benefits to work with. You will find that it is a high-quality library that is going to help us to get things done. You can get it to match up with the libraries that you want, it is going to be free to work with, and it can handle a lot of the data analysis projects that you want to do. It is also an easy library that will connect some of the codes that are already existing in the C language over to the interpreter for Python so you can get your work done.

There are a lot of benefits that are going to come up when you want to work with the NumPy library, and you will find that it is going to be the basis for a lot of the codes and algorithms that you want to write out when you are working with your data analysis. Learning how to use this language and what it is able to do for you is going to make a world of difference in how much you are able to accomplish for the long-term, and it is worth your time to learn more about it as well to complete your project.

Chapter 6: Taking It Further with Pandas

The next option that we need to take a look at is a bit of the work that we are able to do with the Pandas library. This is one of the most important libraries that we are able to work with overall because it is able to handle pretty much all of the parts that come with data analysis. There isn't anything in data analysis that the Pandas library won't be able to help us out with.

Pandas are going to be one of the packages from Python that is able to provide us with numerous different tools to help us with data analysis. The package is going to come with a lot of different structures of data that can be used for the different tasks that we need to do to manipulate our data. It is also going to come with a lot of methods that we are able to invoke for the analysis, which is going to be really useful when we are ready to work on some of our machine learning and data science projects in this language.

As we can imagine already, there are a number of benefits that we can enjoy when we work with the Pandas library, especially when compared to some of the other options out there. First, it is going to present for our data in a manner that is suitable to handle all of our analysis through the different data structures, in particular through the DataFrame and the Series structures.

In addition to this, we are going to find that this is a package that is able to contain a lot of different methods that are going to be convenient for data filtering and more. The Pandas library will come with a lot of the utilities that we need to perform operations of Input and Output in a manner that is seamless. And no matter which format your data is going to come to us in, whether it is CSV, MS Excel, or TSV, the Pandas library is going to be able to handle it for us.

How to Install Pandas

When you work with the traditional Python distribution, you will find that it is not going to have the module of Pandas. You will need to go through the process of installing this to your computer in order to get it to work. The nice thing that you will quickly notice, though, is that Python is going to come with a tool that is known as pip, which is exactly what you want to use in order to install Pandas on your own computer. In order to do this specific installation, we need to go through and use the command below:

$ pip install pandas

If you already have the Anaconda program on your system, then you need to use a slightly different command to help you out. This command is going to be:

$ conda install pandas

It is often recommended that when you do this process, you go through and install the latest version of the Pandas package to get all of the new features and more that we need along the way. However, it is still possible to get some of the older versions, and you can install this one as well. you can just go through and specify which of the versions that you would like to use when working on the conda install code that we did above.

The Data Structures in Pandas

With some of this in mind, it is time for us to go through a few of the different things that we are able to do with the Pandas code. First, we need to look at the data structures. There are two of these data structures that we are able to work with, including the series and the DataFrame.

The first one here is the series. This is going to be similar to what we are able to work with when it comes to a one-dimensional array. It is able to go through and store data of any type. The values of a Pandas Series are going to be mutable, but you will find that the size of our series is going to be immutable, and we are not able to change them later.

The first element in this series is going to be given an index of 0. Then the last element that is going to be found in this kind of index is N-1 because N is going to be the total number of elements that we put into our series. To create one of our own Series in Pandas, we need to first go through the process of importing the package of Pandas through the insert command of Python. The code that we are able to use, including:

Import pandas as pd

Then we can go through and create one of our own Series. We are going to invoke the method of pd.Series() and then pass on the array. This is simple to work with. The code that we are able to use to help us work with this includes:

Series1 = pd.Series([1, 2, 3, 4])

We need to then work with the print statement in order to display the contents of the Series. You can see that when you run this one, you have two columns. The first one is going to be the first one with numbers starting from the index of 0 like we talked about before, and then the second one is going to be the different elements that we added to our series. The first column is going to denote the indexes for the elements.

However, you could end up with an error if you are working with the display Series. The major cause of this error is that the Pandas library is going to take some time to look for the amount of information that is displayed, this means that you need to provide the sys output information. You are also able to go through this with the help of a NumPy array like we talked about earlier. This is why we need to make sure that when we are working with the Pandas library, we also go through and install and use the NumPy library as well.

The second type of data structure that we are able to work with here will include the DataFrames. These are going to often come in as a table. It is going to be able to organize the data into columns and rows, which is going to turn it into a two-dimensional data structure. This means that we have the potential to have columns that are of a different type, and the size of the DataFrame that we want to work with will be mutable, and then it can be modified.

To help us to work with this and create one of our own, we need to either go through and start out a new one from scratch, or we are going to convert other data structures, like the arrays for NumPy into the DataFrame.

There are a lot of different parts that we are able to handle when it comes to the Pandas library. And getting this set up and ready to go for some of our own needs is important in this process as well. this is one of the best libraries to work with when it is time to handle our work with Python coding with data analysis. This can handle all of the different parts that come with the data analysis along the way.

Chapter 7: The Importance of Cleaning and Organizing the Data

Now that we know a bit more about the data analysis and how it is going to work, and how to work with the Python language, it is time for us to work with the first steps that are necessary to handle this process. There are a number of steps that we need to focus on when it comes to handling the data. And this means that we are not going to start out with just creating our algorithms and calling it good. Instead, we need to do a bit of work to gather the data that we want to use, and then we need to be able to clean and organize it in a manner that it will be able to handle the analysis that we want to do.

In this chapter, we are going to take a look at some of the steps that we need to do in order to get started with our own data analysis. There are a few parts that come with this one including setting up our initial questions, looking at the right steps to help us collect the data, exploring how the data works, handling the outliers, and the missing values, along with the duplicates and more. Let's dive in a bit and look at some of the steps that belong to this part of the process.

Collecting the Data

The first step to this process is to actually gather the data that we want to handle. The good news here is that we have a lot of sources that we can use to find our data. We live in a world that has a ton of data right at our fingertips. From asking customers questions about their products, looking at some of the shopping habits of their customers, going through various websites, conducting websites, and more. There is a wealth of information that we are able to use on a regular basis, and learning how to find the data, and making sure that it is high quality so that we can use it correctly in our algorithms.

To start here, we need to have a good idea of what we are looking for when it comes to the data that we want to use. What is your goal in using this data? What are you hoping to accomplish when you have this data, and what is the point of working with the data analysis in the process? This is going to be important because it helps us to make sure that we are actually going to have everything in order and that we search through the right kind of data as we go.

Once we have our direction, it is time to start gathering up the data that you need to make this happen. There are a lot of sources that you are able to rely on based on what you are looking up. Social media is a good place to start. You can also work with online searches, third party surveys and research, focus groups, and more.

Gathering up a lot of data is important. But it is more important to make sure that your data is high-quality. The better the quality of your data, the more that it is going to be there to help our algorithms do well and ensure that we will be able to rely on the different results that we get. It is never a good idea to go through and just use any old data that you can find. This is going to make it impossible to get accurate results, and it will not be worth your time to do the data analysis in the first place.

Organizing the Data

Once we have had a chance to go through and collect all of the data that we need, it is time for us to go through and organize some of the data. If you get it from all of the different sources that we talked about before, it is likely that you will end up with a pretty good mess here. There is a lot of good data that you are able to go through and sort as you go. But it is going to come with missing and duplicate values, in a bunch of different formats, and there are likely to be a ton of outliers and other issues that we need to work with. This is going to make it hard for us to go through and know how to handle the data, and your algorithm will not be able to do anything about this until you can actually go through and organize it.

The first step that we need to work on here is making sure that we are able to get the data as organized as possible along the way. And a good first step here is to sort it out into a common format. Many businesses like to take their data and get it to fit into a spreadsheet or another similar format. This is going to help us to really keep things organized as we go, and can make it a lot easier for us to look it over and have it sorted.

Depending on the kind of data that we are working with, you may find that working with something else or another type of software that we are going to handle. You need to just make sure that the information ends up in the right format. The goal is to get the data to be in the same format so that it behaves and can all go through the different algorithms that you want to work with along the way. This can take some time, but it is going to make your life so much easier as you work through some of the steps that we will do along the way.

Dealing with the Outliers

Another thing that we need to work with here is the outliers. There are some situations where these are going to be useful and can help us to get a lot done and even sow off some new niches and ideas that we have not considered before, but other times, they are just going to be in the way and can skew your results away from some of the real options that you should consider.

In many cases, you will want to ignore the outliers and get rid of them. There will just be a few of them that are way off from the mean or the average that you want to use and can make your results go way over from what they should be. When you look at the data, or even a chart about the data, and you notice that it has just a few pieces or points that do not match up where they should, then it is best to just delete these so they don't mess with the results you should get.

On the other hand, it is always a good idea to take a closer look at the outliers because there are times when they will share important information with you. If you look at these outliers and see there are a number of these outliers that happen to all around the same area, then this could give you some information that can grow your business. It may show you a new niche or a new demographics that you are able to market to and work with.

Sometimes, your outliers are going to be important, so it is at least worth your time to take a look at them and see what you are able to learn. However, keep in mind that these outliers are not always going to matter, and in many cases, they are just going to mess with the results that you get out of your algorithms if you do not get rid of them. Check them out, but be ready to delete them and get rid of them to ensure that you can get accurate results later on.

Filling in Missing Data

There are times when we want to work with our data, and we will notice that there are data points that are missing. When we try to collect our data from a wide variety of sources, this is something that is likely to happen along the way. It is important for us to go through and decide what we want to do with these missing values so that they don't skew the rest of our data and cause issues.

There are a few different methods that we are able to use to make this one work for us. If there are only a few of these options in the data set, then they are probably not that big of a deal, and it is easiest for us to just delete those missing values and not deal with them.

The issue with this one, though, is that there are usually a significant number of values that are missing, or you do not want to delete things if you are just missing one thing in a collection for a customer and the rest of the information is there and can be useful. This is why we will usually need to manipulate the information a bit and see how we are able to make some changes to ensure that this is going to still work for us.

One of the methods that are popular to work with is to take the average of the other similar columns in your data. You can set it up so that if something is missing, have it set up so that you are able to fill it all in wit the average of the other columns. This is a quick and efficient manner of handling some of this information and will help to deal with some of the outliers that we are able to find in our data.

How to Deal with Duplicates

There are times when we are working through our data, and we will end up with a lot of duplicates. There are times when just a few of these are not going to be that big of a deal. But if we are going through and have quite of these duplicates, then there are going to be a few issues along the way. It is going to end up skewing some of the work that we do with the other data in the spreadsheet or the other source that we are working with.

Duplicates are not going to seem like a big issue as we go through the whole process of doing our data analysis. But you will find that if we are able to go through and get through the process of getting rid of the duplicates, then everything is going to work a bit better. Your results will show up in a more accurate manner, and you will be able to get everything to line up during the training and the testing phase as well.

This is why we need to take some time to go through all of our data and eliminate the duplicates as much as possible. You can decide, based on the types of data that you are working with, how many duplicates you will allow. Sometimes it is fine to have a few duplicates in the data, and it is not going to affect things too much. But if you end up with more than that, it is possible to see this happen, and you may not be able to trust your data. Then there are some people who will choose to go through and cut the duplicates down so there are no longer any of these in the data at all.

Cleaning the data that you will use in your own data analysis is something that takes some time. You will find that it actually will take up the most time of all the other processes that we need to handle in our data analysis. This is because the data analysis needs us to have data that is organized and easy to work with. If there are duplicates, missing data, and data that is not that organized, then you will find that the results that you get are not going to be that accurate along the way.

The more time that we are able to spend organizing and getting our data to be as high-quality as possible, the better. This helps to speed up the training and testing process of our algorithms later on and can make it so much easier for us to actually trust the results that we are able to get along the way. This is important if we actually want to use the data analysis to help us make some important and smart decisions along the way, and can ensure that we are able to get ahead of the competition and more. It may not be the most glamorous part of the whole process, but it is one of the most important parts.

Chapter 8: Training, Testing, and Repeating

Now that we have had a chance to spend time looking for the data that we want to use, and that we have had a chance to clean and organize all of our data, it is time to move on to the part that is a bit more fun in the process. It is time for us to look a bit more at the fun part. We are going to look at some of the fun things that we are able to do when it comes to our algorithms and making sure that they are able to provide us with some of the accurate results that we are able to handle with this.

There is actually a good deal of work that we need to do when it comes to working with our algorithms. You can't just push the data through and assume it is going to provide us with a few of the different options that we want along with the way. These algorithms are not going to be set up to provide us with accurate results right off the bat. We need to be able to go through and really look through, doing the training and the testing of the algorithms to help us increase the accuracy. When the accuracy is high enough, only then are we able to go through and really see some amazing results with our algorithms.

With this in mind, let's take a closer look at some of the steps that we need to take in order to get this done, and to ensure that we are able to really get these algorithms to work well in the long run.

Picking Out the Algorithms to Use

The first thing that we need to consider here is which of the different algorithms we are going to use. There are a number of algorithms that we are able to handle. And it is going to take some time to really ensure that we pick out the right one depending on the data that we want to work with, and the types of information that we are working with when it comes to our data.

There are a lot of algorithms that we are able to handle, and they are going to fall under three main styles of machine learning, which is the idea that is going to really push and run our algorithms. These are going to include supervised learning, unsupervised learning, and reinforcement learning.

We are going to explore these in more detail in the next chapter. But we can take a moment to look through these here as well. To start with, we have supervised learning. This is where we are going to show a lot of examples to the algorithm with the right answers to the end. This helps the program to learn from these examples. Then we are able to test it on the knowledge it learns as we go through this process.

Then it is time to work with unsupervised learning. This one is a bit different because we are not going to show the algorithm the results with the example that we use. We expect the program to be able to learn all on its own. Instead, we are going to take the time to have the program learn on its own. This takes a bit more time for the program to learn and gain the right accuracy that we want. But when it gets to this point, you will find that the unsupervised learning is going to be really strong and can take on a lot more options and program capabilities than we will be able to go with all of the other choices.

And then we can move on to what the reinforcement learning. This one is going to take us to another level as well, though, in the beginning, it is going to look like it is pretty much the same as the unsupervised learning that we were talking about above. The main difference that we are going to see with this one is that we will set this up in more of a trial and error kind of method.

Reinforcement learning is going to work on trial and error and will be able to learn when it does things wrong or gets the answer wrong. It will remember all of this and work from there in order to get more accuracy. It learns on its own but has a set of rewards and punishments to help reinforce the kind of learning that we are trying to work with.

All of these can be important in helping us to handle some of the different things that we want to do with our data analysis. Since all of them are different, though, we need to make sure that we are going through and choosing the one that will help us out with our needs.

Take your time when you pick out the algorithms that you want to work with. There are a ton of options, and all of them have benefits and some negatives that you need to work with as well. Learning about some of the different types and how they work will help us to really work through our data and find the results that we want.

Training Our Data

The next thing on the list that we need to explore is how to train our data. It would be nice to pick out the algorithm we want to run, throw the data into it, and then use the results that come out of that, knowing that they are accurate right from the beginning. But this is not the way things actually work. We need to take some time to work with that algorithm and train it to behave well.

This is where we will need to take all of that data that we found and worked through in the last chapter, and split it up. We need to have at least two categories here. We will have one to be in our training set and one that will be a part of our testing set. Each of these is going to have their own roles to follow and can be important to ensure that we are going to be able to teach our algorithms the proper way to behave.

First, we have the training data set. This is the set of data that we are going to use in order to make it easier to teach the algorithm how to behave. We will show the data with the corresponding right answers along with it. This needs to be the set of data that is the highest quality so that we can ensure that the algorithm is going to learn the right information along the way. Take your time to push the data through, maybe even doing it a few times so that the algorithm has more instances where it is able to learn how to behave in the process.

Testing the Data

After we have had some time to train our algorithm, and all of the training data has gone through that chosen algorithm, it is time to do some testing. Using a brand new set of data (remember that we split our data up into two parts in the beginning), we will push the data through the algorithm to see what results we can get.

The accuracy level that we end up with here is going to tell us a lot of information. For example, it is going to let us know whether the algorithm was able to learn along the way, how well it learned, and how much more work we need to do to make this process accurate enough that we are able to rely on it along the way with the data analysis.

When you do the testing part of the process, you want to aim to get above 50 percent. You do not need to get all the way in the 90 or even the 100 percentile, because this is going to happen with time, not with just one training and one testing session. Even if you get a number that is lower, like in the low 60 percent, then this is a good sign.

The assumption when you go through this is that any accuracy that is above 50 percent shows us that the algorithm was able to learn. We assume that even if the algorithm did not have any training at all, and we just jumped right in with the testing, the algorithm should be able to give us some results that are correct, at least half of the time. If you can get an accuracy that is above that, then this is a good sign that your training went well. You may need to go through it a few more times to get the accuracy up a bit more, but this is still a good sign.

If you do this, though and your accuracy ends up below 50 percent, then we have a problem. The algorithm should never get below this much accuracy, and if you are seeing these kinds of numbers, then it is likely that your training went wrong. These numbers are usually indicative of your data is bad, and that you did not get the high-quality data that you should have to start.

With these kinds of numbers, you need to go all the way back to the drawing board. Using the same kind of data to go through the process again is not going to do you or anyone else any good, and it can really cause some harm to the results that you get through this. It is probably best to go out and find some better data, data that is higher in quality. At the very least, you should take the time to rework on your data and make sure that it is going to behave in the manner. Whether this means better organization, checking the missing values, cleaning it more, or picking out a different algorithm, there is something that needs to change when this starts to happen to you.

Hopefully, we do not have that last problem, and instead, we end up with an algorithm that learned something. It may not be as high of accuracy as we would like to start with, but it can be a good start. We will need to go through the process and get it higher, but if you can get any accuracy that is above 50 percent, then pat yourself on the back because you have started off on the right foot in this process.

Repeat the Process

Unfortunately, this is not where it all ends. Unfortunately, getting 60 percent accuracy is not going to be an excuse to walk away and do nothing else with some of the work that you want to handle. It is a good start, but we need to rinse and repeat to get this higher. Our goal here is not to get it to 100 percent. That takes a long time and won't really happen until we put this into some of the real-world applications that we are hoping with these algorithms. However, if you are looking to use this as a way to make decisions and learn more about your industry, it is likely that you want the algorithm to start out with more accuracy than 60 percent.

So, how do we get the accuracy to be higher? We go through the same steps that we outlined above, many times over. When the first test is done, we go through and do another set of training, making sure that the data we rely on is strong and will provide us with the answers that we want. Then, when that training is all done, we go through and do another test, and hope that we are able to get a higher accuracy level in the process.

This is a process that we may have to repeat multiple times in order to get the accuracy that we want. The cool thing about machine learning, though, is that these algorithms are able to learn, and they will get better at some of the work they do. The more data that you feed to them, the more that they are able to learn from that information along the way. And as long as your training and testing data are higher in quality and are on the right topics, you will find that it is going to work in your favor, and the accuracy levels will go up.

The number of times that you need to go through this process will often depend on your own goals and what you are hoping to accomplish. If you want to get the accuracy level up as high as possible before you start working with the algorithm, then you will need to do more iterations of the training and the testing. If having a little bit lower accuracy is fine because you know the algorithm will have plenty of time to learn as it goes, then you may be able to get away with fewer iterations to get this done. It all depends on the kind of project that we are going in the first place.

Working with the different algorithms that are present in data analysis is kind of fun, and is one of the parts of the process that many people are excited to learn how to work with in the first place. When you get to this part, we are finally going through the steps to learn how to make the algorithms behave so that you can use them to make smart business decisions for your needs.

While this part is exciting, it is important to not get ahead of yourself too much here. You still need to take some precautions and think things through to ensure that you are doing it in the proper manner. If you rush through it, the accuracy is not going to be there, and you will not get the algorithms and more to behave in the manner that you would like.

However, this is going to be some of the fun stuff in the data analysis process, and you will quickly find as you work through these algorithms that this is exactly why we needed to take so much time to work on the data organization and cleaning that we talked about before. It will ensure that this part of the process stays fun and that you can actually get some of the accurate results that are so important here.

Chapter 9: Machine Learning and How It Fits Into Our Data Analysis

The next topic that we need to talk about when it comes to data analysis is machine learning. This is going to be an important part of our data analysis because it helps us to work with some of the algorithms and the models that we want to control in this process. With the help of machine learning and the use of the Python language that we talked about earlier, we are able to see our algorithms actually work and do some of the insights and predictions that we want to work with along the way.

To help us see why machine learning can be useful to our data analysis, we need to take a closer look at how machine learning is going to work in the first place.

This chapter is going to take a look at what machine learning is all about, what we can do with it, and some of the different types of machine learning that are important as we go through this.

What is Machine Learning?

The first thing that we need to take a look at here is the basics of machine learning. This is going to be one of the techniques that we can use with data analytics that will help teach a computer how to learn and react on their own, without the interaction of the programmer. Many of the actions that we will train the system to do will be similar to actions that already come naturally to humans, such as learning from experience.

The algorithms that come with machine learning are going to be able to use computational methods in order to learn information right from the data, without having to rely on an equation that is predetermined as its model. The algorithms are going to adaptively improve some of their own performance as the number of samples that we will use for learning will increase.

There are a lot of instances where we are able to use machine learning. With the rise in big data that is available for all industries to use, We will find that machine learning is going to become one of the big techniques that are used to solve a ton of problems in many areas, including the following:

1. Computational finance: This is going to include algorithmic trading, credit scoring, and fraud detection.
2. Computer vision and other parts of image processing. This can be used in some different parts like object detection, motion detection, and face recognition.
3. Computational biology. This is going to be used for a lot of different parts, including

DNA sequencing, drug discovery, and tumor detection.

4. Energy production. This can be used to help with a few different actions like load forecasting and to help predict what the prices will be.
5. Manufacturing, aerospace, and automotive options. This is going to be a great technique to work with when it comes to helping with many parts, including predictive maintenance.
6. Natural language processing: This is going to be the way that we can use machine learning to help with applications of voice recognition.

Machine learning and the algorithms that they control are going to work by finding some natural patterns in the data that you can use, including using it in a manner that will help us to make some better predictions and decisions along the way. They are going to be used on a daily basis by businesses and a lot of different companies in order to make lots of critical decisions.

For example, medical facilities can use this to help them to help diagnose patients. And we will find that there are a lot of media sites that will rely on machine learning in order to sift through the potential of millions of options in order to give recommendations to the users. Retailers can use this as a way to gain some insight into the purchasing behavior of their customers along the way.

There are many reasons that your business is able to consider using machine learning. For example, it is going to be useful if you are working with a task that is complex or one that is going to involve a larger amount of data and a ton of variables, but there isn't an equation or a formula that is out there right now to handle it. For example, some of the times when we want to work with machine learning include:

1. Equations and rules that are hand-written and too complex to work with. This could include some options like speech recognition and face recognition.
2. When you find that the rules that are going to change all of the time. This could be seen in actions lie fraud detection from a large number of transactional records.
3. When you find that the nature of your data is going to change on a constant basis, and the program has to be able to adapt along the way. This could be seen when we work with predicting the trends during shopping when doing energy demand forecasting and even automated trading, to name a few.

As you can see, there are a lot of different things that we are able to do when it comes to machine learning, and pretty much any industry is going to be able to benefit from working with this for their own needs. Machine learning is more complex, but we are able to combine it together with Python in order to get some amazing results in the process and to ensure that our data analysis is going to work the way that we want.

How Does Machine Learning Work with Data Analysis?

Now that we know a little bit more about how machine learning works and why it is important, it is time for us to take a look more specifically at how machine learning is able to come in and help us out with our data analysis. There are so many reasons why we are able to use machine learning when it comes to the data analysis, so it is important to take some time to look at how we can use it as well.

Machine learning is basically going to be the underlying process for all of the algorithms that we want to create along the way. No matter how simple or how complex your algorithm will be, a lot of the coding and the mechanics that come with it are going to really be run by the machine learning that we will talk about in this guidebook. And with the help of Python, you can make some really amazing algorithms that help us to sort through the data.

So, if you are actually hoping to go through this process of data analysis with the goal to sort through your data and understand what is found inside of it, then you need to learn a bit about machine learning ahead of time. The good news with this one is that machine learning is going to be able to work well with the Python language that we talked about above, ensuring that we can get it done with a simple coding language, even though the ideas that come with machine learning are going to be a bit more complex overall.

Supervised Machine Learning

The first type of learning that we need to take a look at here is known as supervised machine learning. This is going to be the most basic form of machine learning that we are able to work with, but it will provide us with some of the different parts that we need in order to keep things going well and can help us to train our algorithms in a quick and efficient manner.

To start, supervised learning is simply going to be the process of helping an algorithm to learn to map an input to a particular output. We are going to spend or time on this one while showing lots of examples, with the corresponding answers, to the algorithm in the hopes that it will find the connections and learn. Then, when the training is done, the algorithm will be able to look at new inputs, without the corresponding output, and give us the right answer on its own.

This whole process is going to be achieved when we work on a labeled data set that was collected earlier. If the mapping is done correctly, the algorithm is going to be able to learn in a successful manner. If it is not reaching the goals here, then that means we have to go through and make some changes to our algorithm to help it learn well. Supervised machine learning algorithms, when they are trained well, will be able to make some good predictions for the new data they get later on in the future.

This is going to be a similar process that we would see with a teacher to student scenario. There is going to be a teacher who is able to guide the student to learn well from books and other materials. The student is then going to be tested and, if they are correct, then the student will pass. If not, then the teacher will change things up and will help the student to learn better, so that they are able to learn from the mistakes that they made in the past so that they get better. This is going to be the basics that come with using supervised machine learning.

Unsupervised Machine Learning

The second type of machine learning that we are able to work with is known as unsupervised learning. This is going to be a method that we can use in data analysis because it will enable the machines to go through and classify both the tangible and intangible objects, without having to go through and provide the machine or the system with any information about of time about the objects.

The things or the objects that our machines are going to need to classify are going to be varied, such as the purchasing behaviors of the customer, some of the patterns of behavior of bacteria, and even things like hacker attacks or fraud happening with a bank. The main idea that we are going to be able to see with this kind of learning is that we want to expose our machines to large volumes of data that are varied and then allowing the algorithm to takes time to learn and infer from the data. However, we need to be able to take the time in order to teach the program how it can learn from that data.

It is pretty common for a computer system to need to learn how to make sense of large volumes of data, both the unstructured and the structured types, and then learn what insights are inside. In reality, it may be almost impossible to provide prior information about all of the data types that a system could receive over a period of time, and working with this kind of machine learning can help to make things happen, even when you are not able to train your machine ahead of time to teach it.

Keeping all of this in mind, we will find that supervised learning is not going to be all that suitable in every case, such as when the systems we are working with need to have a constant amount of information about data that is new. For example, hacking attacks on a bank or a financial system are going to frequently go through and change their patterns and their nature. Supervised learning would struggle with keeping up, but unsupervised learning is going to be more appropriate to handle this.

In these cases and more, unsupervised learning is going to be able to go onto a system and quickly learn from all of the data from the attack to keep up. Then it is able to infer and learn some more insights about potential future attacks, while also suggesting some preemptive actions to work with along the way.

There are a lot of times when we will want to work with unsupervised learning. Any time that you want to work with a program or a machine that needs to do at least a little bit of learning on its own in order to get things done, then unsupervised learning is going to be the right option to focus on.

Reinforcement Machine Learning

The third type of machine learning that we need to take a look at is known as reinforcement machine learning. This is going to be a bit different compared to what we saw with the other two options, but there are a lot of times when we can use this kind of learning to help us out with sorting through our data, including our data analysis. Let's dive into the basics of reinforcement machine learning and how we can use it for our needs.

To start, the reinforcement learning, in the context of artificial intelligence, is going to be a type of dynamic programming that is able to train algorithms, based on the idea of the reward when the algorithm gets the right answer, and a type of punishment when it gets the wrong answer.

One of the algorithms that use reinforcement learning, or the agent, is going to be able to learn how to interact with the environment that is going on around it. The agent or the algorithm is going to receive some kind of reward when it performs in the correct manner. But when it performs incorrectly, it is going to get some kind of punishment or penalty in the process. The agent, through these rewards and penalties, is going to learn, without any kind of intervention from a human, by maximizing its reward and then figuring out the best way to minimize the penalty that it is going to deal with.

The algorithm is going to be successful with this when it has a chance to learn the right way to behave, and the wrong way to behave. When it learns, through the rewards, the right way to behave, it will continue on with those actions or those guesses in order to get more rewards. And when it does get a penalty for doing something wrong, it is going to remember this as well and will learn how to avoid these along the way as well.

Reinforcement learning is going to be one of the approaches that we are able to use with machine learning, and the inspiration for it is going to be found in behaviorist psychology. We can view this in a manner that is similar to how a child is able to learn a new task. This learning is going to have some contrasts to how the other machine learning options will approach a situation because this particular algorithm is not going to be explicitly told how it should perform a task. It has to learn and go through this problem all on its own.

As an agent, which could be something like a program that is set up to play chess or a self-driving car, is going to interact with the environment that is all around it, and it is going to receive a type of reward state depending on how well it is able to perform. So, if the game is able to successfully win the game of chess, then it will receive a reward.

This goes the other way as well. if the agent does not perform in the manner that it should, whether that means that it doesn't win the game when it should, or does something else that is wrong based on the programming, then it is going to get a penalty of some sort. In the case of the game, it is going to be checkmated rather than winning, and it can learn from that in the process.

The agent, through more practice and over time, is going to be able to make some good decisions in order to maximize its rewards and minimize the number of times it gets a penalty through dynamic programming. The advantage of working with this kind of approach, especially when we work with artificial intelligence, is that it is going to allow our AI program to learn without the programming having to go through and spell out exactly how an agent should complete its own tasks.

As we can see, there are a lot of different parts that come together with the idea of machine learning, and being able to explore some of these and what we are able to do with the three main types of machine learning is going to be important based on how we want to use this in our own data analysis. Take some time to look more closely at how we can utilize all of the types of machine learning for our own needs, and move from there into using it to help pick out the algorithm we need to see success.

Chapter 10: Presenting the Results

This guidebook has taken some time to look at the different parts that come with data analysis. We looked at what the data analysis is all about and some of the benefits of working with this data analysis in the process. We took a look at what we can do with the Python coding language and explored some of the codings that we want to do with this language. And then, we went through some of the different steps that we need to explore in order to really see some results with our data analysis.

With all of that behind us, we now have some of the insights and the predictions that we need from all of this analysis. That still leaves us with another problem to deal with. We need to be able to take all of those insights and predictions and then figure out how to present it in a manner that those who are going to use that data, whether it is us, the shareholders, or others who are interested in the data, will be able to use and understand better.

When we get the data out from our algorithms, there is a wealth of information. But often, it is going to come out in a format that does not make a lot of sense if you are not a data scientist. Even if you are, there can be a lot of technical terms, and often we are going to end up with large reports with lots of technical parts that we need to know about.

We can go through and read this information, and there is not necessarily something that is wrong with this process along the way. But we do need to remember that this can be hard to read through, and will slow down some of the processes that we are working on here. We need to find some better methods to present the data, methods that will make it easier for us to look through the data, even at a glance, and understand what is there.

This is where the idea of data visuals is going to come in. There are a number of methods that we can use to help present the data that we want to work with, but nothing is going to be as effective as working with these data visuals. These will help us to sort through some of the insights and predictions that we have found along the way, and can make it so that we can see these connections at just a glance, rather than looking through and hoping that the reports and documents to find the same information.

To keep this simple, data visuals are going to just be a way to present our data in a graphical and pictorial format. It is going to help the decision-makers to see some of the analytics that are presented in a more visual manner, helping us to grasp some of the concepts that are more difficult, and can help us to identify some of the new patterns that are there.

We can even work with some of the visualizations that are out there. These are going to make it so that we can take our data visual process to another level by using a lot of different types of technology to drill down into the graphs and charts into as many details as possible. The interactivity that comes with these is going to make a big difference in the way that we are able to see data, and even in the manner that we process this data.

There are a lot of reasons that we need to be able to go through and use these data visuals. They are one of the best ways for us to go through and really understand the information that we processed through our algorithms as well. due to the method in which the brain is going to process information, working with graphs or charts to help us to visualize some of the larger amounts of complex data is going to be a lot easier than pouring over a lot of reports or spreadsheets in the process.

Compared to some of the other methods that are out there, you will find that these data visuals will be a quick and easy method to use when it is time to convey concepts in a manner that everyone is able to understand. It is even possible to take some of these visuals in order to experiment with some of the different scenarios possible, simply by going through and making some slight adjustments.

There are a number of things that these data visuals are going to be able to help us out with. Some of these will include:

1. They can help us to identify some of the areas that need more of our attention or some improvements.
2. They can make it easier to see which factors are the most likely to influence the behavior of a customer.
3. They will help us to understand where we should place all of our products.

4. They are great at going through and predicting some of the sales volumes that we need to work with along the way.

This brings us to the point of how we are able to use data visuals. No matter the type of industry that we are talking about, how the size of that industry, there are a lot of different types of businesses that are working with data visuals to make their data work better and to make more sense out of their data.

The first way that we are able to utilize these visuals is to make it possible to comprehend a lot of information in a quick manner. By using some of the graphs and charts to represent information for the business, these businesses find that it is easier to see large amounts of data in a clear and cohesive manner, and they will be able to draw some good conclusions from all of that information as well.

In addition, since it is going to be quite a bit faster to take information and analyze it when it turns into a graphical format, rather than having to go through and analyze it through the spreadsheets and documents that were traditionally used, businesses are able to address some of their major problems and answer questions in a more timely manner.

The next thing to work with is how data visuals are going to be able to help us go through and pinpoint some of the emerging trends. When we use these visuals in order to discover some of the trends, both in the market and in our own business, we will find that it is going to give us a good edge over our competition and that alone is going to be enough to help affect the bottom line. It is easier with these visuals to spot some of the outliers, especially the ones that are going to affect the customer churn or the quality of the customer, and then we can actually address them before they become really big issues.

We can also use these visuals to help identify some of the patterns and relationships that are found in our data. Even when we start to work with some of the large amounts of data that is complicated, we will find that they will make more sense when we present them in a graphical manner. With these visuals, it is even possible for a business to recognize the parameters that are there and are highly correlated.

Some of the different correlations that we will see with all of this will be pretty obvious to work with, but there are some that may be a bit more complicated to handle. Identifying these relationships are going to help a company to make plans to focus on the areas that are the most likely to influence the goals that are the most important to their goals.

And finally, we will find that the data visuals we are talking about here are going to be great options that help us to communicate our story in an efficient and fast manner to others. We can work with graphs, charts, and some of the other representatives of our data that are more graphical is going to be an important part of our data analysis because it is going to be really engaging and can help us to get the message out there a lot faster.

Before we get too far with our data visualization, we need to make sure that we are able to lay a bit of the groundwork as well. before we implement a bit of this new technology, there are going to be a number of steps that we have to go through and take. Not only do we want to make sure that we have a nice solid grasp on the data that we are working with and what we hope to see with it in the process, but we also need to have a good idea of our goals, needs, and audience as well.

Being able to prepare our company for this kind of technology is going to take some time and work as well. Some of the parts that have to come with this in order to make it work for our needs include:

1. We need to have a good understanding of the data that we need to visualize. This means that we need to know the size of the data we want to use. We also need to have a better idea of how unique the values in the data area or their cardinality.
2. Then we need to go through and determine the exact thing that we want to be able to visualize and have a good idea of the information type that we are hoping to communicate here.
3. Next, we need to make sure that we know as much about our audience as possible, and that we understand how that audience is going to be able to process all of that visual information.
4. Then we need to end this with a good knowledge of how we will use that visual in a manner that will help us to convey the information in the best form and the easiest form for others to handle as well.

Once we have been able to go through and answer these four questions about the data type that we would like to handle here, and the type of audience who will be looking at the data and the visuals, it is then time for us to go through and do a bit of preparation for the amount of data that we want to work with. Keep in mind that big data is often going to bring about a lot of new challenges to the visuals due to the different varieties that we want to use, the large volumes, and some of the varying velocities that we want to work with as well. Plus, it is also common for the data to get generated at a rate that is faster than we are able to manage it and analyze it, which is going to bring in another challenge to the mix.

There are also a few different factors that we want to handle here and consider to make the visual work. For example, we want to make sure to focus on the cardinality of the columns that we would like to visualize here. When we deal with high cardinality, that means that we will end up with a larger percentage of values in our set of data that are unique. This could be something like a data set of bank account numbers since we would expect each number to be different.

It is also possible for the data set we want to work with to be lower in the cardinality. This means that the column data that we are working with is going to come with a larger number or percentage of values that are able to repeat. This is something that is going to repeat on a frequent basis, such as the gender column in your data set.

While it may be a bit easier for us to go through and grasp some of the concepts that come with these data visuals and how it is going to help us out when it is time to take a lot of data and try to make sense of it. However, it is sometimes harder to understand what should come next and how you can create your own visuals. For example, what kinds of technology are you going to need and how you are able to use it for your needs.

There are a number of tools that we are able to use when it is time to create some of our own data visuals. The Matplotlib extension that works with the Python library is a great option to work with because it allows us to work on pretty much any of the different visuals that we want to handle, from charts and graphs and so much more. Pretty much any of the different options in visuals that you would like to focus on will be available with this library, and it allows you to use the simple Python language, which is going to make things so much easier for you.

Working with these data visuals is going to be important to our data analysis. It may not be the first thing that we think about when we handle some of the data analysis that we want to do here. And it is easy to think that it is not that important to start with. But it can make or break the project that you are handling when you get started.

These visuals are going to help us to go through and really understand what data is found in our algorithms, and instead of having to read through the documents and the spreadsheets that are out there with our insights and data, we can turn it into a visual and understand the complex relationships so much better. Whether we are using this for our own needs or presenting this to the owner of a business and their shareholders, you can't go wrong finishing up your data analysis with the help of some strong data visuals about that information.

Conclusion

Thank you for making it through to the end of *Python for Data Analysis*, I hope it was informative and able to provide you with all of the tools you need to achieve your goals whatever they may be.

The next step is to get started on working with your own data analysis. We spent a lot of time in this guidebook looking at what the data analysis is all about, some of the benefits of this analysis ad why a lot of different companies want to use this for their own needs, and even how to work through the steps of your own data analysis as well. Even as someone who is just getting started with data analysis and learning how to make this work for their own needs, you will find that this guidebook has all of the different tips and tricks and techniques that you need to see success.

In this guidebook, we took the time to look over a lot of the different things that we are able to do when it is time to work with data analysis. We looked at the benefits of the data analysis, some of the steps that we are able to use to get through this analysis and get the results that we want, and even how to work with things like the Python coding language and machine learning to get more out of our analysis as well. When all of this comes together, we are able to really show off our skills and enjoy all of the neat things that come with our analysis in the first place.

When you are ready to learn more about what a data analysis can do for you, and how you are able to work with this data analysis in order to get the best results, along with the Python language and machine learning, then it is time to take a look at what this guidebook has to offer!

Finally, if you found this book useful in any way, a review on Amazon is always appreciated!

www.ingramcontent.com/pod-product-compliance
Lightning Source LLC
Chambersburg PA
CBHW071348210526
45465CB00001B/18